See Him As He Is

SEE HIM
AS HE IS

Author

MICK J. BRINDLE

Copyright© 2012

See Him As He Is
By Mick J. Brindle

Copyright © 2012
Printed In The United States of America.

Unless otherwise noted, Scripture is taken from the HOLY BIBLE NEW INTERNATIONAL VERSION. Copyright© 1973, 1978, 1984 by the International Bible Society. Used by permission of Zondervan Publishing House. All rights reserved.

You may use any part of this book in any manner appropriate, to build up the body of Christ in an effort to reach unity in the faith and the knowledge of the Son of God attaining the whole measure of the fullness of Christ.

Please note, that the name satan and related names are not capitalized. I choose not to acknowledge him, even to the point of violating grammatical rules.

*Copying this material for profit or resale is prohibited.
All rights reserved.*

Table of Contents

Chapter 1 - Free Your Mind — 11
Just around the corner - Come to yourself - Everyone searches - Our mentality - Sight without vision

Chapter 2 - God Is Moving — 31
Better things - Focus your lens - A demonstration of power Stubborn faith - A new movement

Chapter 3 - Reality Shift — 51
Stepping out - Philip and the Ethiopian - Developing intimacy

Chapter 4 - Intimacy — 67
Levels of intimacy - Jesus and His disciples - His workmanship

Chapter 5 - Kingdom Keys — 85
Jesus told Peter - Supernatural keys - Lock and unlock

Chapter 6 - He Said Go — 105
Healing came - One word - I understand them

Chapter 7 - The Stirring — 117
Provision provided - Church perspectives - For the one

Chapter 8 - On the Road   133
You're important to God – A lighting strike – Cancer healed

Chapter 9 – Generous Mercy   147
Tears of desperation – Puppy love – Saved at 77

Chapter 10 – Wounded Warriors   159
God's Glory - God allowed - A new norm – Renewing the mind - Conclusion

Introduction

As children of light, our first and foremost pursuit is to seek the face of God, to seek His presence. This should be the inner desire of our heart; to develop and nurture an intimate relationship with our Savior. It's God's deepest desire as well for us to do so.

Oh, dear children of mine, have you realized it? Here and now we are God's children. We don't know what we shall become in the future. We only know that, if reality were to break through, we should reflect his likeness, for we should see him as he really is! 1 John 3:2

When I read this verse, the words *"we shall see Him as He really is"* struck me. What exactly does that mean? Although this is referring to Christ's return, how do we really see Him in our daily and spiritual lives? When we have an encounter with God, when we see Him at work, how does this change us?

What I've noticed is this; when people experience, when they encounter God, the event changes the way they view life and their relationship with Him. There's this awakening that impacts their lives both spiritually and physically.

It's when He reveals Himself in such a way, that there comes an infusion of just how real He is. We have an encounter with His depth of love and encouragement for our life and future.

It's when you have a personal encounter with God that your level of His reality becomes more real to you. In other words, you come to a supernatural understanding both mentally and spiritually of His enormity and grandeur. How does this occur? In His presence, He reestablishes your perception of what was really meant to be normal. When this occurs you experience a glimpse, a revelation of the true personage of God. You have a revelation of a new revealed truth that overpowers a previous experience, taught behavior, or what you have previously thought was true. In many ways you come to realize what you thought was normal, really wasn't.

What's apparent today is a lack of pursuing the power and presence of God, but especially His Spirit. When you read the New Testament the Holy Spirit was supposed to change everything; so that this gathering of people who call themselves Christians, had this supernatural element about them, the power of the Spirit. But in these days, can you really tell the difference between believers and non-believers? Do you see His supernatural power at work in the church and in the life of His people?

It's in the encounter with the Lord that we are transformed to become more like Him. It's in these encounters that we "see Him as He really is" in the moment. Amazingly, these encounters become life altering events in our spiritual maturity.

As you read each chapter, you may notice that one builds upon the other. You may come to realize something new you haven't thought of before. God may reveal to you what I call, *kingdom truths*. They may even seem somewhat radical. But you know what; we have a radically revealing God!

Chapter 1

FREE YOUR MIND

For God gave us a spirit not of fear but of power and love and self-control. 2 Tim 1:7

Just Around the Corner

In our ministry we help the homeless and poor who are struggling daily to survive. Monthly we assist several thousand people who are trying desperately to live life. Our goal is to encourage them in any way we can with food and clothing to help make ends meet. Occasionally we have the opportunity to go deeper in relationship with someone willing to let us share in their personal situation.

We have a homeless lady who has been coming to the ministry for over seven years. She left her hometown and relocated to Abilene in search of a job, but unfortunately was not able to find one.

As a result she ended up living on the streets and homeless camps in the woods for most of those years. She came to the ministry most every day for five years. When we opened our new clothing building one of my staff members invited her to come and volunteer. Over time this staff member developed a close relationship with her. As a result she started volunteering and did so for over two years.

What you need to understand is, this lady was at times hard in her approach to others. Her manner and speech was difficult for others to understand. They weren't aware of the hardships she went through or the things she was forced to endure while living on the streets. It was truly a difficult and desperate lifestyle for her to live in.

Her mind was set in survival mode most of the time because of her situation and the environment she was in. As a result, this behavior and speech for her became normal. Her way of thinking was much different from those she interacted with in the ministry.

Each morning before opening, we pray and have a devotion time. After several months of nurturing and being around Godly people I started to notice a change. She continued to come every day for several years. She shared with me how desperate she was to get off the streets and to live a life without fear. I kept telling her, *your blessing is right around the corner*.

Eventually I had the opportunity to share Jesus with her and after two years I was privileged to baptize her and several others in our parking lot with many of our homeless as witnesses. I kept telling her, *your blessing is right around the corner*.

We have a house in a neighborhood near the ministry that was used by college students as an outreach to the community. Well the students graduated and moved on. One thing led to another and we were able to give her that two bedroom house. Through the generosity of one of our church supporters we were also in a position to hire her at the ministry. She is now off the streets, a homeowner, and working on staff! Her blessing came. Praise the Lord!

She is not the person we once knew seven years ago. How did this happen? I strongly believe it was because of her "willingness" to serve God. He intervened and changed her life. You see, her mind is being renewed. She was set free from the bondage of poverty because she started to believe her blessing was right around the corner. It was the positive reinforcement of my staff; those speaking life into her and sharing the love of Christ that helped change her mindset. She was set free! God restored to her His place of blessing and *she saw Him as He really is!*

Come To Yourself

You see, God wants to renew, to change the perspective of your mind. The devil is holding people captive by their head, by their mind, and if the devil has your head, he has you.

In Luke 15: 12, we see a similar story about a father who had two sons. The youngest son went to his father and said, "Give me my portion of the property, my inheritance."

His father of course granted his request. Little did the son know, that in his father's wisdom, life would teach him a valuable lesson.

Soon after, he took the money from all he owned and headed out to a distant country, a journey of great excitement, so he thought! Unfortunately he soon got caught up in the lifestyle (entangled in the chains of that culture) and wasted all that he had on loose living. He soon found himself in a desperate situation. He was penniless, homeless, and starving.

In our life, because of our own desires, and sometimes our own decisions, we create chains (entanglements) that ultimately affect our relationship with God and others. That's when we find ourselves in a desperate situation, just like this young son.

This young man found himself estranged from his family, there's no doubt about it. He was hated by his brother because of his selfish request. His father's heart longed for him to return home. He spent his inheritance on foolish worldly things, there's no doubt about it. He was starving; working a menial, dirty job, in the hog pen of life. He was empty (physically) and utterly depraved (spiritually).

He was living like hell, hanging around cursed objects and his mind reverted back to the lusts of the flesh, the old carnal mind, there's no doubt about that. When he indulged in the influence of a sinful culture, he lost "control"; control of his behavior, control of his possessions, control of his self-worth, and control of his "mind."

There he was, at the lowest point in his life, and then Luke 15:17 says, "He came to his senses", he came to "himself." The deception lifted and he was once again in his right mind.

"When he came to his senses, he said, 'How many of my father's hired servants have food to spare, and here I am starving to death!" Luke 15: 17

For God did not give us a spirit of timidity (of cowardice, of craven and cringing and fawning fear), but [He has given us a spirit] of power and of love and of calm and well-balanced mind and discipline and self-control." 2 Tim 1:7 (Amplified)

He returned to his father's house asking for forgiveness. He returned to the place of blessing. You see, he realized his selfish decision brought only desperation and death.

LET'S BE REAL

He was a son who was living like a servant. In Luke 15:29 we see the older brother who simply considered himself to be just another one of his father's servants.

This makes one consider if he was doing it for love, or was it just good business? When you read verse 12, you might discover that the father didn't just give the younger brother his share; but he gave both sons what they had coming to them. He said, "All I have is yours".

The older brother was very wealthy in his own right. Unfortunately, somewhere along the line, he had become his work.

Don't forget, as a child of the King, you to have been very wealthy from the beginning.

"But we had to celebrate and be glad, because this brother of yours was dead and is alive again; he was lost and is found." Luke 15:32

More than anything you guard, protect your mind, for life flows from it. Proverbs 4:33

His mind was renewed, it was transformed, he was set free and the chains were broken. What he experienced, the patterns of the world were overwritten with what is good and once again acceptable to God. He had a new lease on life, a renewed "perspective."

"Do not be conformed to this world (this age), [fashioned after and adapted to its external, superficial customs], but be transformed (changed) by the [entire] renewal of your mind [by its new ideals and its new attitude], so that you may prove [for yourselves] what is the good and acceptable and perfect will of God, even the thing which is good and acceptable and perfect [in His sight for you]." Rom 12:2 (Amplified)

There are many today, maybe even you, who have strayed away from God for one reason or another. But I want you to know, it's always His desire that you return to His place of blessing. It's the Father heart of God that longs for you. He stands waiting as a loving Father for His children's return.

Everyone Searches

Isaiah wrote, *"My soul yearns for you in the night; in the morning my spirit longs for you"*... Isaiah 26:9

At some point in life I truly believe everyone searches for God in one way or another. Honestly, some become more desperate for Him than others. It's the heart's desire of our loving Father that we long for His presence and power in our life and ministry.

> *We should be expecting big things from God. He wants us to be willing to engage people right where they are in life. Regardless of the situation, it must be an expectation of every believer to see God at work. To see Him as He is.*

It's His longing that our relationship with Him would be:

- ✓ **Authentic**
- ✓ **And Alive!**

Look at Isaiah. He was considered the most highly educated of all the prophets. He was both intelligent and articulate in all that he wrote. With the exception of Daniel, he possibly occupied the most influential position of all the prophets as well. Isaiah was a God seeker, he yearned for God.

What I've witnessed in our church culture today, is a diminished yearning for the presence and power of God's Spirit; for most unfortunately a mindset of self-sufficiency. If you haven't noticed, in America the availability of resources often dominates our need for God, or need for divine intervention.

Let's Go Deeper: It's when we experience the power of God that the *"linkage"* between the believer and the indwelling power of the Spirit grows stronger and more real. Over the years I've noticed as this occurs, there's a transformation that brings about a deeper hunger for things of the kingdom. God's love breaks the chains of the prodigal. His love restores blessing and prosperity.

It's in the encounter with the power of His Spirit that brings breakthroughs in our walk with God, and what I call, *"the unshackling"* of the Holy Spirit in our lives." A shifting of our perspective occurs and when this happens normalcy is restored. Our perspective is renewed.

In this process we come to the understanding that we don't get more of the Holy Spirit in quantity, but we do receive "more" in the sense of relationship and power when we give Him freedom in our lives. This occurs as we grow closer in our relationship with the Lord. We come to rely more and more on Him.

Isaiah was a "God-seeker." He knew the importance of coming into and living in God's presence. He knew that living in God's presence was the single most important part of his life.

His Spirit

God is omnipresent, meaning that He is everywhere at all time. David said in Psalm 139:7, *"Where could I go from Your Spirit? Or where could I flee from Your Presence?"* He concludes that there is no place that we can hide from the presence of His Spirit.

Although the Holy Spirit is always with us, there are times when His presence is closer and more obvious. Our closeness however, is a result of our willingness to seek Him, to allow Him into our lives.

It involves seeking Him in every circumstance of life, the good and the undesirable. The manifest presence of God is what brings the power of His Spirit. God's manifest presence changes lives and reveals His glory.

People often tell me, "I just don't experience or see the power of God working in these days." My reply to them is always this, "do you expect Him to, are you seeking Him?"

You see, God reveals Himself to those that earnestly seek Him (Deuteronomy 4:29). If we hope to walk in the power of His Spirit, then we should be practicing the presence of God.

> *In other words: Acting accordingly because we know God's Spirit is with us, in every moment.*

The Holy Spirit Comes

"When the day of Pentecost came, they were all together in one place.

Suddenly a sound like the blowing of a violent wind came from heaven and filled the whole house where they were sitting.

They saw what seemed to be tongues of fire that separated and came to rest on each of them. All of them were filled with the Holy Spirit and began to speak in other tongues as the Spirit enabled them.

Now there were staying in Jerusalem God-fearing Jews from every nation under heaven. When they heard this sound, a crowd came together in bewilderment, because each one heard their own language being spoken.

Utterly amazed, they asked: "Aren't all these who are speaking Galileans? Then how is it that each of us hears them in our native language?" Acts 2:1-8

When the Spirit came upon them, there was a release of incredible power. The result was tremendous and the New Testament church was born. It's this same release of power the apostles received at Pentecost, which God expects for every believer to walk in today!

Jesus said, "But you will receive power when the Holy Spirit comes on you… Acts 1:8.

The same power that conquered the grave lives within each one of us! But do we believe it?

Our Mentality

Think about the mentality of the Israelites, still stuck in the Egyptian mindset after Moses led them to freedom. Even after they witnessed the miracles, signs, and wonders that secured their release, they still longed for Egypt. Why, because their minds were still "shackled" to the past. They remained focused on their current circumstance. They remained entangled in Egyptian culture just as did the prodigal son.

Here is our struggle today! The church is deceived with tradition and ritualism. Most simply act out what they were taught being a Christian should be, instead of realizing what our identity in Christ reveals. In other words, many have either never known, or have been led away from who they truly are in Christ. They have no identity.

For the Israelites, it's all they had known for 430 years. They were acting out what they were conditioned and taught to do. Internally they longed for what was safe and most familiar. Isn't that what most do today?

Sight without Vision

Helen Keller was once asked, what would be worse than being born blind, and she said, "To have sight, without vision." In other words: to live life without the expectation of something greater. To miss the opportunity of stepping into the unknown, the future.

You see, they had no vision, no purpose in life.

Even though the presence of God was with them in the pillar of cloud and the pillar of fire, they still feared. They longed for the life of a slave because of the chains formed while in captivity. They were unable to see beyond their immediate circumstance because the chains of unbelief, the unknown brought a spirit of fear.

*"When Pharaoh drew near, the Israelites looked up, and behold, the Egyptians were marching after them; and the Israelites were exceedingly **frightened** and cried out to the Lord. And they said to Moses, Is it because there are no graves in Egypt that you have taken us away to die in the wilderness?*

Why have you treated us this way and brought us out of Egypt? Did we not tell you in Egypt let us alone; let us serve the Egyptians? For it would have been better for us to serve the Egyptians than to die in the wilderness." Exodus 14: 10-12

What really stuck with me was this: The same is found today. People are dragging around chains from the past that dominate their God-given purpose in life. It's these "unhealthy" chains, those bonds that keep us from moving forward into the future God has pre-destined for each of us. In the minds of the Israelites all they had to look forward to was death. Their only expectation was to die in the wilderness.

God breaks off generational chains.

✓ **We are a chosen generation!**
✓ **We walk in the power of the Spirit!**

> *We're all chained in some way! Often it's those things we don't want others to know about. The secret struggles in our lives.*

Eph. 2:10 says: "For we are God's handiwork, recreated in Christ Jesus, that we may do those good works which God predestined (planned beforehand) for us to do, that we should walk in them [living the good life which He prearranged and made ready for us to live]." (Amplified)

Gal. 5:25 says, "Since we live by the Spirit, let us keep in step with the Spirit."

Smith Wigglesworth, a famous revivalist of the early 1900's once said, "I'm a thousand times bigger on the inside, than I am on the outside." What he was referring to was his walk with the Spirit. He had an expectation that God would do greater things with his life.

Question: What does it mean to live by and walk in the Spirit?

It means we must be prepared and attentive to what the Spirit wants to do, "in the moment" with great expectation. More importantly, we must be willing to embrace His calling on our life! Why? Because, the Lord tells me, "bigger and better things are yet to come."

He wants us unchained from those things holding us back, allowing Him to show us how to live the life He intended, full, abundant, and free.

The Holy Spirit has absolute power and authority, but it's important to understand that He *voluntarily steps back.* He wants us to willingly cooperate and to partner with Him.

LET'S BE REAL

Penetrating deeply to our commitment to Christ is the question.

Do we know God is working all things to our good?

Sometimes in this life we have the rare privilege of seeing just how God uses setback and disappointment.

We recognize the wisdom and strength that comes through walking with His Spirit, and witness how He helps us overcome the obstacles in life.

Do we have all the answers? No. But living and walking with God is part of the adventure knowing He does!

God delights in knowing that we press through the difficulties in life, trusting Him. We do this because we know He is much bigger than we ourselves could ever be on our own!

Coming is a new season of power; the moving of the Spirit in a way not experienced since the book of Acts. Why? Because God is starting to move! He's breaking off the old religious mentality, and moving us towards a renewed reality, as you will see in the chapters to follow.

Things to Think About

- ✓ Are there hindrances that keep you from God's blessing?
- ✓ Are you practicing the presence of God daily?
- ✓ Do you long for God's vision and plan for your life?

Chapter 2

GOD IS MOVING

For the LORD your God moves about in your camp to protect you and to deliver your enemies to you. Your camp must be holy, so that he will not see among you anything indecent and turn away from you. Deut 23:14

God is beginning to move in a way that has not been witnessed in the last century. He's restoring families, marriages, health, prosperity, and hope. The amazing thing is this; He's doing it in and through His people.

We are living in a time, in a generation that's beginning once again to realize the power and benefit of the spiritual gifts in this modern day. More and more the body of Christ is engaging the power of the Spirit for the restoration of the church through the gifts of the Spirit. I can't help but know the gifts are intended to minister to the body of Christ, to bring restoration as in the beginning.

I see Him restoring the mentality of the early church. He is restoring the focus and the provision of the kingdom through a *new revelation of truth*. He is setting in motion a plan to move forward with a new surge of power through the Holy Spirit in the days ahead; for this generation and the next to come.

We are called as believers to be forthright and engaged. There's a new call to purity and holiness in every aspect of our lives. He's restoring what was lost to the enemy and delivering him to us as we overcome deception with truth.

Better Things

God continually prepares us for even "bigger and better things." As we see once again in the book of Exodus, the Israelites didn't embrace what God had in store for their future. When Moses led them out of Egypt, all they wanted was to return. God doesn't want us, nor did He want the Israelites to be content with their spiritual position. He doesn't want us to remain in a situation that hinders advancement of the kingdom.

The goal is to continually move forward towards the future. Just as with the Israelites, He wants us to let go of the golden calves in our lives, those entanglements that keep holding us back. He wants us to overcome those strongholds we deal with daily and move forward in freedom.

Why? Because we have a:

- ✓ **Moving God**
- ✓ **An advancing God**
- ✓ **And a loving God**

It's God's intention, His purpose that we participate in a greater plan that advances kingdom work. It's in this expectation for us that we continually move forward, and as we encounter Him daily, we grow spiritually. The more we see Him as He really is, the more frequently we encounter His glory. It's in the pursuit that we grow, becoming more like Him.

Beloved, we are God's children now, and what we will be has not yet appeared; but we know that when he appears we shall be like him, because we shall **see him as he is***. 1 John 3:2 (ESV)*

Although this verse is referring to Christ's return, I believe if we just step out of our theological grid, we will see that it is applicable even for today. I will expound more on this in chapter 7.

We can't remain attached to the idols and hurts of the past. When we do, the joy meant for our future is lost. Holding onto these things will only hinder what God intended us to fully become. The deception of the enemy starts in the mind and must be "resisted." His only purpose is to kill, steal and destroy, robbing us of our joy and freedom.

Submit yourselves, then, to God. Resist the devil, and he will flee from you. James 4:7

As mentioned previously, if we don't have a joyful expectation that something good will occur in our Christian walk, a chain of bondage may exist. This diminishes our faith in God and in the power of His Spirit in our life. Why, because we see our situation as hopeless.

> ## LET'S BE REAL
>
> *We're all going to face problems. Wouldn't you rather face them with an army of fellow believers who are like minded and encouraged by the Holy Spirit every step of the way?*
>
> *I don't know about you, but I have no desire to associate with those who constantly bring up past defeats. Our God is on the move and He expects us to move with Him in victory. Our God is a revealer. He revels Himself in His plan for eternity and for each one of us!*
>
> *He reveals new truth, new revelation, and renews our mind.*
>
> *I personally don't have time to give consideration to the devil because my focus is on the kingdom. The devil focuses on the past and the present because he knows he has no future.*
>
> *Where's your focus?*

Hopelessness can hinder our effectiveness to minister to others because we soon become consumed with our own circumstances. This can and often does, lead to unforgiveness as well as bitterness towards others.

What we must realize is that our identity is in Christ and Him alone! When we allow the Spirit to bring freedom into our lives we have the opportunity to lead others to freedom as well. We have the opportunity to share the victory we have in overcoming our life challenges with others.

I mention this because: Our spiritual position (our state of mind) will have an effect on our ability to move in power and to engage what God has planned for us, our purpose in this life.

Like many today, the mindset of living in Egypt became comfortable. Living the life of a slave was normal. They feared what was different. They had no point of reference for the bigger and better things God had in-store for them. Unfortunately, many today are living the life of a slave not realizing Jesus came to establish freedom for the oppressed.

> *It's the same today. We have been conditioned to think and act a certain way.*

"The Spirit of the Lord is on me, because he has anointed me to proclaim good news to the poor. He has sent me to proclaim freedom for the prisoners and recovery of sight for the blind, to set the oppressed free... Luke 4:18

The longer you live in bondage, the more living in this condition becomes what is perceived as normal. How wonderful would it be to just let go of past hurts or disappointments and move forward into the greater things God has for us. It's possible, but requires a willing faith on our part.

Breaking this link requires us to unclench our fist; letting go of the past and opening our hand to receive the future.

- ✓ **Past:** Everything we experienced and were taught. We cling to them because it's what we are secure in.
- ✓ **Future:** Brings a sense of uncertainty. Why, because we have not yet experienced it, the unknown, the unexpected.

Focus Your Lens

It's so incredible when we break free. Our minds then become increasingly receptive to the things of the Spirit. Our earthly lens goes beyond the natural. *(What we've been taught)* By God's Spirit, through love and freedom, He changes our perception to accept things beyond the natural; the supernatural, the future!

That's when we realize:

- ✓ You can't move into the greater things of God if continue to think as you always have.
- ✓ You can't put new "vision" new "revelation" or new "blessings" into an old way of thinking. The old mind can't retain them.

Let's Go Deeper: It's because of the presence of His Spirit within us that exists the potential to view life through a lens that exceeds the boundaries of this earth. It's the Spirit that changes us from our natural condition (thinking and perception) to a kingdom-minded position (expecting the kingdom to come in power). When this occurs, it creates a shift in our reality. Why, **because God reveals Himself** in the shifting.

That's when our faith and expectations become anchored in the "eternal." We start to think and act based on what the Word of God says a result should be, instead of relying on the circumstances to determine the outcome. ***This becomes a revelation of a new revealed truth.*** What's even more amazing is; you recognize the shifting. Recognizing what God is doing indicates progression in your walk with His Spirit. It's advancing towards the future!

More and more we come to the understanding that our natural perceptions shouldn't dictate any situation we find ourselves in. It's the Word of God that reveals what our position should be in every circumstance.

It's our authority through Christ that has been provided to bind anything contrary to the kingdom and release everything that's appropriate and lawful.

Jesus said, "I will give you the keys of the kingdom of heaven; whatever you bind on earth will be bound in heaven, and whatever you loose on earth will be loosed in heaven." Matt 16:19

It's His might, strength, and authority that enables us to handle the anointing of power placed upon us.

Hebrews 1:9 says: "You have loved righteousness and hated wickedness; therefore God, your God, has set you above your companions by anointing you with the oil of joy."

God's gifts and His call on your life are irrevocable. Rom 11:29

A Demonstration of Power

We should expect to see God move because we "**seek**" Him, we "**invite**" Him to "**show**" Himself.

So many today miss out on the glory of God because they don't expect God to move in power. They don't "seek" after the deeper things of the Spirit (especially the giftings) in their personal or corporate faith.

As I said before, in a way many within the body today have lost perspective and purpose!

For Example: When it comes to the power of the Spirit, what's the difference between the church of Acts, and the church of today?

In Acts they:

- ✓ **Lived it.**
- ✓ **Experienced it.**
- ✓ **Expected it.**
- ✓ **Witnessed it.**

They had purpose! In the mind-set of the early church the power of the Holy Spirit was "real." It's because their minds were set on the kingdom. (Col 3:2)

Today, because many haven't experienced the Holy Spirit's power, they don't believe. They have not yet encountered this new dimension of faith. Why, because it comes by a ***demonstration of power.***

*I came to you in weakness with great fear and trembling. My message and my preaching were not with wise and persuasive words, but with a **demonstration** of the Spirit's **power**, so that your **faith** might not rest on human wisdom, but on God's power. 1 Cor 2: 3-5*

For the kingdom of God is not a matter of talk but of power. 1 Cor 4:20

Walmart Revival

This is probably one of my favorite encounters with the power of the Spirit. If there's one thing I've discovered it's this; God is all about giving us *opportunities* to do something out of the ordinary. Some of you may not know this, but God often uses you to change people's lives in some of the strangest ways through a demonstration of His power.

One evening not long ago I had to run to Walmart to pick up a few items. As I first walked into the store, immediately there was an anxiousness in my spirit. I felt like jumping right out of my skin. I know many of you know what I'm talking about. I just knew God was going to do something that involved me and it was going to be a little strange. Now you may be wondering what I mean by that. In Isaiah 28:21 it speaks of *"His strange work."* Gods work can seem at times very strange to many.

Upon entering the store I started praying and talking to the Lord asking; ok Lord, how are you going to weird me out this time! I started off on my hunt picking up the things I needed and at the same time there was great anticipation building as I waited for the Holy Spirit to do what He had planned. As I shopped I first noticed an elderly lady with a cane, but didn't really sense anything. Then my attention was drawn to this large gentleman, but nothing came. As I found the last item my attention was drawn to another lady, you guessed it, nothing! Making my way to the checkout counter I noticed how very crowded it was, which is pretty typical for Walmart.

About now I'm thinking this whole thing must have just been my imagination. As I approached the front I saw a checkout lane with no one in it, so of course that's where I headed. I'm thinking again, well maybe I missed the opportunity with those three people my attention was drawn to earlier.

I can honestly admit my enthusiasm was a little dashed at this point. As I placed my items on the conveyer belt, I noticed the young lady at the register had some sort of brace on her right wrist. Ah ha! Well I'm kicking into fervent prayer mode and thinking this must be it, right Lord! I engaged her in conversation and asked what was wrong with her wrist. She said she had carpal tunnel and was about to have surgery.

I asked if it was ok to pray for her to see if God would heal her wrist. She said ok. As she was scanning my items I touched her brace and prayed a simple prayer. Wrist, be healed in Jesus name.

Suddenly she stopped what she was doing and started moving her wrist in the brace. I asked what was going on and she said, "My wrist feels warm all over." I said God is healing your wrist. I asked her to take off the brace and as she did, she started really flexing her wrist even more. Again I asked what was happening and she started laughing and said, "All the pain is gone." Well I'm thinking praise God now I know that's why I came, right! Wrong! About that time I felt a tap on my shoulder. As I turned you will never guess who was standing there. It was the little old lady with the cane. Now I'm thinking, ok God this is really getting weird. She said, "I saw what you did for her" and then she asked if I would pray for her knee.

She explained that several years ago she was in a car accident and had multiple operations. I said absolutely, then touched her shoulder and prayed. She started flexing and bending her knee and said, "It's getting warm all over." She then handed me the cane and started walking around in circles. Shortly afterwards the tears came, as she was crying she said, "After all these years the pain is finally gone!"

Then I felt another tap on my shoulder and it was the large gentlemen I noticed earlier as well. He said, "I damaged my shoulder in an accident years ago and can't raise my arm above my shoulder, will you pray for me too?" I said absolutely, then touched his shoulder and prayed.

He said, "My shoulder is warm" and he started moving his arm up and down flapping like a bird eventually lifting it straight up in the air. I'm thinking "wow" God, you are so awesome.

As I turned to complete my transaction, yep, you guessed it, another tap. It was the other lady I saw as well. She said, "I don't know who you are, but will you pray for me too?" I have migraines and have a really bad one right now. Again, I prayed and commanded the pain and migraines to be permanently removed. After a few moments she started smiling and said, "The pain is completely gone." Praise the Lord!

By the way, the young lady checking me out stopped what she was doing and was watching these events unfold before her eyes. She had tears rolling down her cheeks and hands cupped over her face.

There were people laughing, crying, flapping their arms, and walking in circles at this checkout lane. Is this crazy or what? As you might imagine we drew just a little attention from other onlookers. About this time one of the supervisors came to the register and asked what was going on.

As I walked away from the commotion with my small bag of items I could hear the cashier say, *"You wouldn't believe me if told you, it's something you would have to see."*

Unknown to her, this comment was remarkably very profound. Jesus basically said the same thing.

Jesus said in John 4:48 "Unless you people see signs and wonders," (a demonstration of power) Jesus told him, "you will never believe." (Emphasis added)

Stubborn Faith

Even the apostles "refused" to believe. Although they witnessed first-hand the power Jesus possessed, they stubbornly refused to believe the eyewitness accounts of Jesus after His resurrection.

I'm sure they thought Jesus would have revealed Himself to them before anyone else!

"Later Jesus appeared to the Eleven as they were eating; he rebuked them for their lack of faith and their stubborn refusal to believe those who had seen him after he had risen." Mark 16:14

We must understand it's not about self importance or saying, "look" what I have or what I'm "doing", but about recognizing what God has provided. It's about seeing Him as He really is and becoming more like Him.

And we all, who with unveiled faces contemplate the Lord's glory, are being transformed into his image with ever-increasing glory, which comes from the Lord, who is the Spirit. 2 Cor 3:18

Life is about focusing and pursuing Gods will and presence. As God starts moving in your life, it's very easy to lose focus and start thinking you are more than what "He" made you to be. God gives grace to those who are truly humble as they serve the body, walking with purpose, and with the power of His Spirit. He increases our faith through the outpouring of His favor, as we serve and minister to others. The Lord's entire ministry was about serving others. He came not to be served, but to serve, even to the point of giving His life for us. (Matt 20:28)

For the LORD God is a sun and shield; the LORD bestows favor and honor; no good thing does he withhold from those whose walk is blameless. Psalm 84:11

A New Movement

There is a new movement taking place in this age. The Spirit is renewing the mind-set of the church body.

There is emerging a new thought transformation that ushers in freedom and the unhindered presence of His Spirit.

God wants to move His people into this new dimension of faith. There are blessings He wants to pour into the life of the church. He wants His Spirit released in our lives.

Let's Go Deeper: What we must understand is this; you can't receive new blessings with an old mind; a progressive renewal must take place. The old thought mentality can't retain or embrace a revelation (a revealing) of new truth. How will this occur? Understanding comes as a result of the encounter. It's in these events that the kingdom comes with a demonstration of power. How does this occur? When we pursue Him!

Smith Wigglesworth, known as the "Apostle of Faith" a healing revivalist of the latter 18 and early 1900's once said, "I appeal to you to keep moving on with God into an ever increasing realization of His infinite purpose in Christ Jesus for His redeemed ones until you are filled unto all the fullness of God."

"The child of God must catch the vision anew every day. Every day the child of God must be moved more and more by the Holy Ghost. The child of God must come into line with the power of heaven so that he knows that God has his hand upon him."

"I see people from time to time very slack, cold, and indifferent; but after they get filled with the Holy Spirit they become ablaze for God. I believe that God's ministers are to be flames of fire; nothing less than flames; nothing less than mighty instruments with burning messages, with a heart full of love, with such a depth of consecration that God has taken full charge of the body and it exists only that it may manifest the glory of God."

Things to Think About

- ✓ Are there struggles from your past/present that hold you back in areas of your life? What are they?
- ✓ Do you yearn for an encounter with God's presence? In what way?
- ✓ Do you long to see the power of the Spirit in your Christian walk?
- ✓ Do you long for a new dimension in your relationship with Christ?

Chapter 3

Reality Shift

At once Jesus realized that power had gone out from him. He turned around in the crowd and asked, "Who touched my clothes?" Mark 5:30

This verse is referring to a woman who had a perpetual issue of blood all her life. Such a condition would be difficult for any woman of any era. But for a Jewess, nothing could be worse. No part of her life was unaffected. Sexually, she could not touch her husband. Maternally, she could not bear children. Domestically, anything she touched was considered unclean. Spiritually, she was not allowed to enter the temple.

She was considered a bruised reed. She awoke daily in a body that no one wanted. She was down to her last prayer and on the day we encounter her, she is about to pray it. By the time she gets to Jesus, He is surrounded by people.

He was on His way to help the daughter of Jairus, the most important man in the community. In her desperation she prays her last prayer. *"If I can just touch His clothes, I will be healed."*

> She encountered Jesus and experienced a "reality shift" that changed her life!

What choice does she have? All she has is a crazy hunch that Jesus can help and a high hope that He will. She longed for His response but didn't know if He would. All she knew was that He was good. Now that's faith!

Let's Go Deeper: You see faith is not the belief that God will do what you want. Faith is the belief that God will do what's right. A healthy lady never would have appreciated the power of a touch from the hem of His robe. But this woman was sick and when her dilemma met His compassion, a miracle, a shifting occurred.

Her part in the healing was very small. All she did was extend her arm through the crowd. "If only I can touch him." That should be the cry of our hearts as well. Healing begins when we do something, when we reach out, when we move forward in a simple act of faith!

Do you desire a new shift "a touch" in your Christian walk? Are you open to changing your perspective, the way you view life and your God-given authority? Are you prepared to meet future challenges? Are you dissatisfied with a business as usual approach to kingdom matters and faith?

Normal life is what the world offers, not what God wants most for you. Many voices will be quick to inform you about "you", but there's only one you can trust!

God knows who you are and where He wants to take you, but you need a "shift" in your thinking to go there. More importantly, you must trust His voice instead of all the voices telling you not to.

It's so important to take time to be still and listen to what He's saying and then be willing to move just as she did. This takes place often in a circumstance of desperation. It also takes place when we take a serious approach in our individual commitment to His direction, His voice, and His desires.

Now is the time of reconnection to the power of the kingdom. God is starting to make a shift in preparation for new things He wants to release.

For us it means moving into a place of deeper intimacy. When we do, the shifting will occur.

So many of us walk out Christianity doing what we perceive is right. We do the outward things adhering to what we've been taught or experienced. This makes up what we believe Christian life should be.

We go to church, bible studies, gatherings and everything that goes along with it, but still miss the deeper things God wants to reveal. We want to feel normal. But what does normal look like? I can assure you, true Christian living is anything but normal, especially from a world view. To feel "normal" is the kind of life you're convinced to settle for because everything you hear and see encourages it.

The "normal" voices of life want to inform you, shape you, and define your boundaries. They say this is all you'll ever have and the best you can ever hope for.

The voices tell you that you're not smart or talented enough for anything else. They want you to believe no one really cares about you.

There are two spiritual shifts, but only one is worth pursuing. There are two kinds of voices, but only one can be trusted, your Creator's voice!

LET'S BE REAL

More times than I'm willing to admit many have come to me and expressed their opinions about what they agree with or not in church today.

Unfortunately there are many who simply go through the motions and act the part of what they want others to perceive them to be.

The reason why so many are critical and lack grace is because they are trying to fit into this new club. What they're doing is faking an experience you really had.

One day to their surprise, many will stand before the Lord and share all the things they did for the kingdom, and Jesus will ask the question:

Who Are You? *In other words, we have no relationship; I don't know who you are!*

Where do you stand?

A reality shift doesn't occur apart from a revealed truth. Believers know the source of all truth is the Word of God, but your habit of consuming and conforming to God's Word sets the level of change and understanding you accept or yield to.

Meaning: *When you're exposed to a new truth that challenges a previous experience or teaching, it's called a reality shift.*

> *If you consume His Word superficially, your faith will be superficial. You won't accept change because of a lack of understanding in the depths of His truths.*

When God creates a shift in our perspective, it becomes a life changing event. You may not realize this, but the first time this occurred was when you received Christ as Savior, a shift occurred. He moved you from the path of destruction to one that leads to life. Prior to your salvation you were living in darkness, you were governed by the voices of this world.

What you once perceived (the old way) is now brought into the Light of a new truth (new life). His life, His truth, His way!

"Therefore, if anyone is in Christ, he is a new creation; the old has gone, the new has come." 2 Cor 5:17

This is the eternal shift, the first of many to come as you walk with and develop intimacy in your relationship with the Lord and His Spirit.

We see an example in Matt 14:29. "Come," he said. Then Peter got down out of the boat, walked on the water and came toward Jesus." Matthew 14:29

Stepping Out

When Jesus said come, step off the boat and into the sea, Peter was given an opportunity to change his perspective from the known (Present) to the unknown (Future).

Peter was a fisherman. He was fully aware and knowledgeable about the capabilities of the boat in any situation. Everything he was taught and knew was on the boat. In the open sea Peter knew it was a place of safety, a place of comfort, and a place where he had some measure of control.

He stood and saw a figure far off and asked, is that you Lord? If it is, call me to come to you. Jesus said, "Come!" Then Peter stepped down off the boat and into the water and began to walk towards Jesus.

Peter stepped away from everything he knew, his place of comfort, his place of control and understanding. He stepped out of the realm of the natural and into the supernatural, the future where Jesus had control.

When this occurred, Peter experienced a *"shift in his reality."* He had an encounter with Jesus that resulted in a revelation of a new revealed truth. The supernatural power of God then became personal.

Great acts of faith are not often born out of calm calculation. It wasn't logic that caused Moses to raise his staff at the bank of the Red Sea.

> *It's when he took his eyes off Jesus, his (perception shifted) his reality reverted back to the (natural) and he began to sink!*
>
> *His natural tendency was to rely on his previously know experience and teaching.*

It wasn't common sense that caused Paul to abandon the law and embrace grace. And it wasn't a confident committee that prayed in a small room in Jerusalem for Peter's release from prison. But it was a fearful, desperate, band of backed-into-a-corner believers who had faith enough to expect God to move in their situation, just as Peter did.

God reveals new truths to each one of us in a personal way many times in our relationship with Him. When this occurs, it changes you to become more and more like Him. It's in those moments that you see Him, as He really is! Why, because you have *relinquished control.*

Philip and the Ethiopian

In Acts chapter 8 we see a remarkable example of a shift in perspective.

*Now an angel of the Lord said to Philip, "Go south to the road – the desert road – that goes down from Jerusalem to Gaza." So he started out, and on his way he met an Ethiopian eunuch, an important official in charge of all the treasury of the Kandake (which means "queen of the Ethiopians"). This man had gone to Jerusalem to worship, and on his way home was sitting in his chariot reading the Book of Isaiah the prophet. The Spirit told Philip, "Go to that chariot and **stay near it**."*

Here we see the Holy Spirit presenting Philip with a moment of opportunity. He was obviously being set up. He had no idea what was in store for him in the next few hours.

Then Philip ran up to the chariot and heard the man reading Isaiah the prophet. "Do you understand what you are reading?" Philip asked.

"How can I," he said, "unless someone explains it to me?" So he invited Philip to come up and sit with him. This is the passage of Scripture the eunuch was reading:

"He was led like a sheep to the slaughter, and as a lamb before its shearer is silent, so he did not open his mouth.

In his humiliation he was deprived of justice. Who can speak of his descendants? For his life was taken from the earth."

The eunuch asked Philip, "Tell me, please, who is the prophet talking about, himself or someone else?" Then Philip began with that very passage of Scripture and told him the good news about Jesus.

He received Christ as Savior.

As they traveled along the road, they came to some water and the eunuch said, "Look, here is water. What can stand in the way of my being baptized?" And he gave orders to stop the chariot. Then both Philip and the eunuch went down into the water and Philip baptized him.

When they came up out of the water, **the Spirit of the Lord suddenly took Philip away***, and the eunuch did not see him again, but went on his way rejoicing. Philip, however,* **appeared at Azotus** *and traveled about, preaching the gospel in all the towns until he reached Caesarea.*

Can you imagine what the two of them must have thought? Philip was transported some 50 miles from where he was, appearing outside the city of Azotus. Both Philip and the Ethiopian experienced a (reality shift). One had their eyes opened to the truth of Christ and the other the supernatural power of God!

Phillip was transported from the physical into the spiritual and then back to the physical. You see, God is not bound by the laws of physics, they are bound by Him!

Developing Intimacy

What I've noticed is a "longing" in the body of Christ for the supernatural. We all crave it, but many have difficulty in pursuing it.

Why? Because too few realize what the craving is actually for. Most know there is something missing in their relationship with Christ, but can't put their finger on what it is.

That's why so many feel lonely, empty, or unfulfilled, even though they appear to have every reason to feel the opposite.

There's emptiness, because of a lack of intimacy with God and His transforming power in their life. They don't really know Him because they lack the (mind) of Christ!

Paul addresses church leaders in Corinth. They were infant believers who were not yet mature enough to understand the mind of Christ. They were still pursuing worldly things, much like today.

Brothers and sisters, I could not address you as people who live by the Spirit but as people who are still worldly – mere infants in Christ. I gave you milk, not solid food, for you were not yet ready for it. Indeed, you are still not ready. You are still worldly. 1 Cor 3: 1-2

God wants us to live an abundant, joyful life. He has good plans for our future; plans to bring us hope.

That's why God created within us this craving for intimacy, to have a relationship with Him. He gives us the ability to become over-comers. He gives us the ability to see through the deceptions of the enemy.

- ✓ Who told you you're defeated?
- ✓ Who told you that you would never amount to anything?
- ✓ Who said you couldn't pray for people to be healed?
- ✓ Who told you that you can't break that addiction?
- ✓ Who told you, you were lacking in anything?

It's when you have a personal encounter with God that your level of "His" reality comes to the forefront. He becomes more real to you through His way of thinking. He re-establishes in your mind what kingdom truth is. When this occurs your inner spirit craves more of Him because of a new spiritual stirring.

Why, because of the supernatural connection with His Spirit. Kingdom truth reveals the superficiality of past experience and previous wrong teaching.

We all need to grasp hold of this. It's God's intention that we be:

- ✓ Over-comer's
- ✓ Victorious
- ✓ Successful
- ✓ Healthy

- ✓ Prosperous
- ✓ Empowered

He was very intentional about these things, if not; He would never have said it! If He didn't pre-ordain it, He would never have sent His Son to die for it!

I know this sounds deep, but simply put, without God we are an empty shell lacking any real purpose in this life. Without intimacy we just go through the motions of what we perceive and were taught a Christian ought to be!

> *People without God are only a part of what He intended them to be. If you're not living out God's plan for your life, you won't reach the full potential of what He has in plan for you.*

Things to Think About

- ✓ Are you searching for a new dimension of Christian living?
- ✓ Has what you've experienced and were taught as a believer in Christ come up short?
- ✓ Are you desperate for the transforming power of God in your life?
- ✓ Are you ready for a reality shift?

Chapter 4

INTIMACY

I do not cease to give thanks for you, remembering you in my prayers, that the God of our Lord Jesus Christ, the Father of glory, may give you the Spirit of wisdom and of revelation in the knowledge of him, having the eyes of your hearts enlightened, that you may know what is the hope to which he has called you…
Eph 1: 16-18

Something Special

One Sunday morning the prayer team went forward as we normally do. I really sensed something special was going to happen. As I waited there many others came forward and were being prayed for. I think I was the only one not praying with someone, but then a young lady came down the center isle headed straight for me. As I watched her approach, the Lord gave me a vision of her with children all around. In this vision she was in the center of a large crowd of them and they were all hugging her and reaching out to her. Often God will give me visions, a picture, or words to impart to people coming for prayer.

As she came up to me, we introduced ourselves and I asked her what she would like prayer for. She simply said, "I just want God's direction in my life." We spoke for a few minutes about other things, but I just knew God had something big for this young lady.

I asked if it was ok to anoint her with oil and she said she would love that. I told her I normally wait a few minutes to see what God wants to share. As I waited, He showed me the children again and a word flashed in my mind; it was "Mozambique." As I waited, I also saw her in a classroom studying with a number of other young people just like her. The Lord then showed me a pair of pants with holes in the knees. This is often how He reveals to me a person that either has a dedicated prayer life, or has been praying for direction and confirmation of something.

As I started praying, I told her the Lord showed me she was a college student studying elementary education. As I told her this I heard a soft sob starting. I also explained how I saw many small children around her and that she loved them very much. I revealed that God has called her to minister to them. She really started crying now with tears flowing uncontrollably at this point. I also shared that she has been praying for a confirmation of her calling and was seeking God's approval.

As I finished, she told me everything I said was true. She was praying and seeking Gods direction and conformation for her calling. She has a heart for young elementary age children and was told by a friend that God wanted her to go on a missionary trip. I then told her the Lord showed me the word "Mozambique." She then looked completely astonished and said that was the word her friend told her as well. I then shared with her the vision I had as she approached me, and in this vision the children I saw were African, not white!

How does this happen? It happens because of intimacy. It's when you have an intimate relationship with the Lord he reveals things to you. In this case, they were things He wanted me to speak into another's life.

Let's Go Deeper: There are deep things to discover that will open us to a revelation of kingdom truths through teaching and demonstrations of power by the Spirit. Both Scripture and experience teach that it's we, not God, who determines the degree of relationship that can be enjoyed. We are at this moment as close to God as we truly choose to be.

"And I am convinced and sure of this very thing, that He Who began a good work in you will continue until the day of Jesus Christ [right up to the time of His return], developing [that good work] and perfecting and bringing it to full completion in you." Philip 1:6 (Amplified)

The more intimate your relationship becomes with God, the more He will reveal His divine purpose for your life.

"But if one loves God truly [with affectionate reverence, prompt obedience, and grateful recognition of His blessing], he is known by God [recognized as worthy of His intimacy and love, and he is owned by Him]." 1 Cor 8:3 (Amplified)

"But there is a God in heaven who reveals secrets, and He has made known to King Nebuchadnezzar what it is that shall be in the latter days (at the end of days). Your dream and the visions in your head upon your bed are these:" Dan 2:28 (Amplified)

Pursuing intimacy requires a willingness on our part to not settle for a less demanding level of Christian living. It's in the nature of our earthly dwelling, our flesh to willingly diminish our commitment. Unfortunately, when we do this, we are in essence hindering the Spirit by not allowing God to use us fully for His purpose and plan.

Everything in our Christian life and service flows from our relationship with God. If we are not in close fellowship with Him, everything else becomes out of balance, we lose our focus. However, when communion with Him is close and real, it's possible to experience a deeper friendship.

I no longer call you servants, because a servant does not know his master's business. Instead, I have called you friends, for everything that I learned from my Father I have made known to you. John 15:15

*"And the scripture was fulfilled that says, "Abraham believed God, and it was credited to him as righteousness," and he was called God's **friend**." James 2:23*

In both the Old and New Testaments, there are examples of close intimacy experienced by God's people. In the Old Testament, it was Moses and the nation of Israel with their God.

In the New Testament, it was that of the disciples and Jesus. In each case, the growing intimacy arose out of a deepening revelation of divine character. The following is a brief summary of their deepening relationship.

> *God loves His servants very much, but one of His greatest desires is to call them "Friend."*

First Level

On several occasions God summoned Moses to ascend Mount Sinai to have fellowship with Him. Twice, the conference lasted for forty days. On one of those occasions, the people of the nation were with him. A study of the circumstances reveals different levels of intimacy.

As the Law was about to be given, God told Moses to prepare the nation for His manifestation on Mount Sinai. They would see His visible presence, but there were limits beyond which they must not pass.

"And the LORD said to Moses, "Go to the people and consecrate them today and tomorrow. Have them wash their clothes and be ready by the third day, because on that day the LORD will come down on Mount Sinai in the sight of all the people… Exodus 19: 10-12

In Exodus 24:2, Moses was the only one that could approach the Lord. The Elders and leaders could only worship from a distance. Moses was the messenger from God to the people.

Why was Moses so exclusive? The reactions of the people then, just as today, clearly demonstrated that they didn't have a desire to come closer to God. (Exodus 20: 18-21)

This sounds all too familiar. Obviously, there were conditions for a fresh revelation of God and a shifting of their perspective, but they weren't willing to pursue it.

They did have a vision of God, but to them "the glory of God was like a consuming fire on the mountain top." In other words, they had a reverence for God, but there was no relationship. (Exodus 24:17)

Second Level

This group pressed past the barriers that excluded the rest of the people and experienced a much more intimate encounter with God than the others. "Under His feet they saw what appeared to be a pavement of sapphire, as clear as the sky itself." Prior to this, they had a limited vision of God and His Glory, but now they gazed upon His eternal splendor.

In Exodus 24 it states; *"they saw God and they ate and drank."* They were literally in His presence. Their experience was far advanced of that of the people, but unfortunately, there was no permanent transformation. They didn't come to a full realization of who God is.

> *The calf represents our perception of past experience: those things in our lives that take God's place. They keep us chained to the familiar.*

He revealed Himself, but their minds were unable to receive Him. This became obvious, because as you know, a short time later they were found worshipping the golden calf.

Third Level

The numbers quickly dwindled as the mountain path grew steeper! Of all Israel, only two qualified for inclusion in the third level of intimacy, Moses and Joshua. What was Joshua's special qualification for that privilege?

A clue is given in Exodus 33:10-11: Whenever the people saw the pillar of cloud standing at the entrance to the tent, they all stood and worshiped, each at the entrance to his tent. The LORD would speak to Moses face to face, as a man speaks with his friend. Then Moses would return to the camp, but his young aide Joshua son of Nun did not leave the tent.

> *Joshua experienced God's presence. He saw Him as He is really is and as a result craved a relationship of deepening intimacy, one of friendship.*

The tent was the place where the Shekinah glory rested and where God manifested Himself to His people. "Joshua... would not depart from the tent." As Moses' servant, he had many duties, errands and services to perform. However, whenever he was free from those duties, he made his way to the tent.

Joshua longed to be in God's presence. We can conclude that he was present on many occasions when the Lord spoke to Moses face to face. Joshua knew what it was like to be in the Lords presence from his experience as Moses' assistant. He enjoyed an intimacy with God excelled only by that of his leader.

Friendship Level

Moses was called into the presence of the Lord. This certainty filled Moses with awe of the living God as he climbed the mountain alone disappearing into the cloud.

You see, the people in the outer circle saw only the consuming fire and feared. Moses saw through the fire and in it the glory of God. He worshipped for forty days and nights. (Exodus 24:15-17)

What would happen if we all experienced the awe and the divinity of the living God and longed to remain in His presence? In many ways we do, but just don't realize there is much more to God than what we don't see.

When God's Spirit speaks to you, when He reveals Himself, that's when you know you are part of the friendship circle!

The Lord would speak to Moses face to face as one speaks to a friend. Exodus 33:11

Dr. J. Elder Cumming contended "in almost every case the beginning of new blessing is a new revelation of the character of God - more beautiful, more wonderful, and more precious." This was certainly true in the case of Moses.

What I've discovered is this; when our spiritual lives move into a place of deepening intimacy, He will empower us with a greater anointing for ministry. He places favor on our lives.

For example: Jesus on the Mount of Transfiguration, and Moses' face before the Lord glowed brightly with the Glory of God. God's presence, His anointing was on them in power!

Jesus and His Disciples

In His ministry, Jesus chose twelve men as the forerunners of the New Testament church. Within the twelve there emerged a circle of three with whom Jesus became especially intimate. They were closer to Him than the others.

Within the circle of three, there was one who appropriated the special place on Jesus' breast, and through whom the disciples channeled questions to the Master. "He leaning back thus on Jesus' breast", (John 13:25) is the way John described his privileged position. Each of the disciples was as close to Jesus as he chose to be.

On four special occasions, Jesus admitted them to experiences from which they learned precious lessons.

First, on the occasion of the raising of Jairus' daughter (Luke 8:51), they were granted a preview of their Lord's mastery over death and saw His gentleness with the little girl. (A reality shift)

Second, on the mount of transfiguration (Matt 17:1), they gained clearer insight into the importance of His impending death, although they grasped its significance very inadequately (Luke 18:34). There too, they had a preview of His glory and majesty. "We beheld His glory," recalled John (John 1:14). "We were eyewitnesses of His majesty," said Peter (2 Pet 1:16). (A reality shift)

Third, on the Mount of Olives (Mark 13:3), they marveled at His prophetic discernment as He shared with them the divine purposes and the inner secrets of God. (A reality shift)

Finally, in the Garden of Gethsemane (Matt. 26:37), they had a glimpse of the sufferings of their Savior and the cost of their salvation. (A reality shift)

Those were some of the privileges of the inner circle. Their relationship with Him was the result of their own choice. It's a sobering thought that we too are as close to Christ as we really want to be.

The deepening intimacy of the three with Jesus was the result of the depth of their response to His love and training. They recognized that intimacy with Him involved responsibility as well as privilege.

The Master told them, *"Whoever does the will of God, he is My brother and sister and mother"* (Mark 3:35). There are some ties that are closer even than those of kinship.

Why then was John the primary apostle in the group?

It was love that drew John into a deeper intimacy with Jesus than the other apostles. John alone possessed the title **"the disciple whom Jesus loved."** If Jesus loved John more, it was because John loved Him more!

LET'S BE REAL

*Christ meets you outside the throne room, takes you by the hand, and walks you into the presence of God. Upon entering we find **grace**, not condemnation; **mercy**, not punishment. Where we would never be granted an audience with the King, we are now welcomed into His presence.*

It's by our relationship with the Son that we gain access to the Father.

Jesus promised, "All who stand before others and say they believe in me, I will say before my Father in heaven that they belong to me." Matt 10:32

Why, because you are a friend of God. With that comes the privilege of entry and access to the throne room.

Mutual love and confidence are the keys to developing intimacy. It would seem that entrance into the inner circle of deepening intimacy is the outcome of our deep desire.

Only those who count such intimacy a prize worth sacrificing anything else for, are likely to attain it. If other intimacies are more desirable to us, it's unlikely we will gain entry.

The place on Jesus' breast is still vacant and open to any who are willing to go beyond the superficial. It's the same in any relationship. We are now, and we will be in the future, only as intimate as we really desire to be.

My wife and I have known each other since high school and have been married 34 years. We know each other so well, our thoughts and what we are about to say are almost always the same. We know the inner desires of each other's heart's and one another's deepest passion's. How can this be? It's because of the time and commitment taken to develop a deepening relationship. Our lives have literally become one.

It's the same in your relationship with the Lord. If you want to know Him on a deep "awe" inspiring level, it takes commitment to develop the relationship. The key is your willingness to just take time to know Him! That's when the love relationship grows. That's when His passion, His desires, and His unbound love become a part of what He designed you to be. As He is!

His Workmanship

This is a season of new things. The Lord wants to have an intimate awe-inspiring relationship with His children. Don't let the distractions of life and this world get in the way of what He has to offer.

Embrace the "shifting" He brings in your life. Engage the "new perspective," the paradigm of change, and walk in the power of His Spirit. We are His workmanship, created to be a part of His plan, bringing truth and encouragement to those who live in desperation.

I can assure you, there will be many encounters in your walk with the Lord. When they come, just as Peter's did, step out of the boat and into the higher calling God has for you. When you do, expect a release of something new and exciting in your life.

Much dreaming and many words are meaningless. Therefore stand in awe of God. Ecclesiastes 5:7

Things to Think About

- ✓ Are you as close to God as you really desire to be?
- ✓ Have you wanted to commit to a deeper relationship with Him, but just don't know how?
- ✓ Do you know what God's plan is for your life, your life calling?

Chapter 5

Kingdom Keys

I will give you the keys of the kingdom of heaven; whatever you bind on earth will be bound in heaven, and whatever you loose on earth will be loosed in heaven." Matthew 16:19

For many years I served God primarily out of duty and without any real purpose. I really didn't know about the power of His Spirit that resided within me. I read about Jesus' ministry and all the things He did, but really had no understanding of what was available to me as a child of the King. We as God's children, as royalty, have been given access to every provision in the kingdom. With this title comes the privilege of entry, unhindered entry. Let's take a look at two sets of supernatural keys.

- ✓ **The First Set Are Those Given - To Us.**
- ✓ **The Second Set Are Those Keys Only Jesus Holds.**

You're probably wondering, what are these "keys"? The key to God's kingdom is first and foremost the Gospel message that brings one to Christ, and through Christ we receive eternal salvation. Remember Christ is the "door" to the kingdom of God.

In John 10:9 (TEV), Jesus said, "I am the door, whoever comes in by Me will be saved; he will come in and go out, and find pasture [spiritual food]."

Christ gave the Church, through Peter, the "keys" that can lock and unlock doors on earth and in heaven. The keys are the entire Gospel message preached, including the authority each of us has in Christ Jesus.

The word "Keys" appears in the Bible only twice.

I have a whole bunch of keys on my key ring. I have keys to my house, the car, ministry buildings, mailboxes and much more. I even have keys that I have no idea what they go to.

Now, I don't know about you, but there's nothing more frustrating for me, than to go unlock a door and don't have the right key. But I have a solution to that problem. You know what it is?

That's right, I make spares. They're not on my key ring, but pre-positioned right where I know they should be. There's another set of keys I have possession of that aren't on my ring. I don't' have them in my pocket, nor are they hidden around the house. They are a supernatural set of keys, keys to the kingdom of heaven, keys you can't see until they're used.

These keys give access by their activation. There's a kingdom truth we all need to really grasp hold of. In Jesus' ministry; as He healed the sick, made the deaf to hear, the blind see, the lame walk, the mute speak, cast out demons, raised the dead, is it possible He was pre-positioning (establishing access) giving us privilege to the keys of the kingdom demonstrated by His actions?

Why do I suggest this? Because Jesus said, "I only do what I see my Father doing." When the Father was putting kingdom keys in-place, could it be that at the same time, Jesus was putting in-place the supernatural connection on earth through a demonstration of His actions while ministering to others?

Jesus gave them this answer: "Very truly I tell you, the Son can do nothing by himself; he can do only what he sees his Father doing, because whatever the Father does the Son also does. John 5:19

These supernatural keys would later be passed on to the apostles, as well as to you and me. He placed into motion His strategy for the future church. He was setting things in-place. Why? Because He said He was going to His Father (John 14:12). He was pre-positioning supernatural keys for our appointed time in history. He was laying the foundation for us to use kingdom keys. God is all about establishing foundations, boundaries, and prepping (planning) for the future.

By wisdom the LORD laid the earth's <u>foundations</u>, by understanding he set the heavens <u>in place</u>; Proverbs 3:19

And he is not served by human hands, as if he needed anything. Rather, he himself gives everyone life and breath and everything else. From one man he made all the nations, that they should inhabit the whole earth; and he marked out their <u>appointed times in history</u> and the boundaries of their lands. Acts 17: 25-26

Jesus knew that after His crucifixion, He would spend a short time on this earth before His final departure. He knew the kingdom keys needed to be pre-positioned, set in-place prior to His crucifixion for our appointed time in history. Why? To be activated in the future by you and me!
He also knew the apostles and others needed to test drive the keys and through personal experience come to the awareness of their access to the power and resource of the kingdom.

The seventy-two returned with joy and said, "Lord, even the demons submit to us in your name."

He replied, "I saw Satan fall like lightning from heaven. I have given you authority to trample on snakes and scorpions and to overcome all the power of the enemy; nothing will harm you. However, do not rejoice that the spirits submit to you, but rejoice that your names are written in heaven."

At that time Jesus, <u>full of joy</u> through the Holy Spirit, said, "I praise you, Father, Lord of heaven and earth, because you have hidden these things from the wise and learned, and revealed them to little children. Yes, Father, for this is what you were pleased to do. Luke 10: 18-21

How you have fallen from heaven, morning star, son of the dawn! You have been cast down to the earth, you who once laid low the nations! Isaiah 14:12

> **This event depicts the original picture of satan being thrown out of heaven.**

It amazes me that when we engage and use our authority in Jesus, it gives Him great joy to see us step into our calling. It's because we are privileged, we have access to the hidden things of God, whereas others do not.

Jesus told Peter

"I will give you the keys of the kingdom of heaven; whatever you bind on earth will be bound in heaven, and whatever you loose on earth will be loosed in heaven." Matthew 16:19

We bind and loose from the earth, not from heaven. Jesus did the same as the God-man. That's why He did what He did, to give us an example, a demonstration of His ministry with power.

If I have a key it means that I have been given authority or access. If I give you a key to my home, you have authority to enter my home. If I give you the keys to my car, you have the authority to drive my car. We have been given the keys (the power of access) to the kingdom through the authority of Christ. The word "keys" in Matt 16:19 is plural, meaning more than one!

When you step into your calling and insert the key to your mind, you unlock a door to a greater reality of God. Set before us are a multitude of doors from every dimension of heaven that reveals great mystery. These keys of authority unlock or (unbind) that which is lawful and appropriate providing for every need in any situation, including healing. The keys also bind anything that comes against the kingdom. Kingdom keys unlock the provision of heaven to be loosed into this natural realm through our actions in ministry. God uses ordinary people, you and I, to fulfill His purpose and plan.

And he said to them, "Truly I tell you, some who are standing here will not taste death before they see that the kingdom of God has come with power." Mark 9:1

Jesus wasn't so much talking about the physical kingdom. More so He was speaking of the manifestation (the appearing) of the kingdom on earth as it is in heaven through the release of supernatural kingdom resources.

Jesus sends out 72 common people to surrounding towns. Jesus says to them:

Whenever you go into a town and they receive and accept and welcome you, eat what is set before you; and heal the sick in it and say to them, ***The kingdom of God has come close to you.*** *Luke 10:8-9*

In other words, when miracles, signs, and wonders occur, the kingdom provision has come on earth as it is in heaven! The keys Jesus gave to Peter, as well as to us, served two purposes:

- ✓ What was bound (or locked up) on earth will be bound in heaven.
- ✓ And that which was loosed (or unlocked) on earth, will be loosed in heaven.

The Keys were pre-positioned.

| **On Earth** | **From Heaven** |
| WE LOCK (Bind): | RELEASED: (Loosed) |

Sickness — Health
Disease — Healing
Physical Disabilities — Restoration (wholeness)
Spiritual Influence — Deliverance
Bondage — Freedom

Jesus came to earth to set the captives free – He didn't do it from heaven. Why? To set the example by His actions – so we would do the same!

- ✓ In Acts 2, on the day of Pentecost, the Holy Spirit came upon the apostles and they began to speak in languages they'd never spoken.
- ✓ A large crowd gathered to see this new thing and guess who stands up to preach a sermon? That's right, Peter.
- ✓ 3000 people received salvation that day and were baptized.
- ✓ Several days later, Peter and John are going to the Temple to pray when they met and healed a crippled man.

Then Peter said, "Look at us!" So the man gave them his attention, expecting to get something from them. Then Peter said, "Silver or gold I do not have, but what I do have I give you. In the name of Jesus Christ of Nazareth, walk." Acts 3: 4-6

- ✓ Peter uses the key of healing to bind brokenness and (unlocks the kingdom) restoring the lame.
- ✓ Again large crowds gather - and guess who stands up to preach? That's right: Peter.
- ✓ Peter used a key of boldness to preach the Word of Truth and the church grew to more than 5000.
- ✓ In Acts 3, Peter walked down the street and when his shadow touched others they were healed instantly.

Nevertheless, more and more men and women believed in the Lord and were added to their number. As a result, people brought the sick into the streets and laid them on beds and mats so that at least Peter's shadow might fall on some of them as he passed by. Crowds gathered also from the towns around Jerusalem, bringing their sick and those tormented by impure spirits, and all of them were healed. Acts 5:14-16

- ✓ In Acts 10, Peter is sent by God to the household of a Roman Centurion to preach to him and to a large crowd of Gentiles who gathered at his home.
- ✓ Before the day was done, Peter and his friends baptized every person in the audience.

Why did Jesus give keys to Peter?

- ✓ Because He knew Peter would "use them."
- ✓ Why did He provide the same keys to us, because He expects us to use them?

Again and again in the book of Acts, Peter was the "point man."

- ✓ Peter opened doors for the crowd at Pentecost.
- ✓ He opens the doors for the crowd at the Temple.
- ✓ And he opened the doors for the crowd at Cornelius' home.

But Peter wasn't the only follower of Christ given permission to bind and loose, to lock and unlock.

- ✓ Peter might have opened the doors at Pentecost.
- ✓ But Philip opened the door for salvation in Samaria.
- ✓ Paul, Barnabas, Silas, Timothy and Titus opened the doors in Greece and Turkey.
- ✓ Matthew opened the door in Ethiopia.
- ✓ And Thomas opened the door in India.

And since those early days, many brave missionaries as well as others just like you and me have opened the doors for millions of people to hear about the love and forgiveness of God through the blood of Christ.

Peter had keys and so do we. Those same keys have been given, granting authority by the King of kings and Lord of lords to unlock every kingdom resource.

Now what does this mean? It means we have the power to unlock (release) and lock (bind) things. It means we have the ability to unlock doors for people to come to Christ and receive healing, just as the apostles did through the power of the Holy Spirit!

They may have big names, but their keys were no bigger than ours. We're in a battle against satan who is our enemy and the keys given to us have power over him bringing daily victories.

Jesus said: "Upon this rock (of Peter's testimony that Jesus was the Christ, the Son of the Living God) I will build my church, and the gates of hell shall not prevail against it" Matthew 16:18

Now the odd thing about Jesus' statement was this: Gates don't attack, they swing on hinges. So, if the gates of hell aren't attacking us, what does it mean for Jesus to say "... *the gates of hell will not overcome/prevail against (the church)?*"

It means that one of the reasons Jesus created the church was to "attack" the gates of hell. He intended for us to take the fight to the enemy, to restore things in His name. We (the church) are the tool (or key) that God intends to use to tear down strongholds. The eternal battle was won when Jesus rose victorious over death and hell, but the daily conflicts rage on. Why, because the devil knows his time is short.

The church is a training ground for war, but it's unlike any war fought on this earth.

*Paul writes: "The weapons we fight with are not the weapons of the world. On the contrary, they have **divine power** to **demolish strongholds**. We demolish arguments and every pretension that sets itself up against the knowledge of God, and we take captive every thought to make it obedient to Christ." II Corinthians 10:4-5*

I mentioned earlier, the things we struggle with, the battles we face daily are directly related to our thoughts. The battle starts in the mind. Satan creates locks in our thoughts that foster doubt and diminish faith. The good news is this; the power of kingdom keys negates satan's bonds.

The mind governed by the flesh is death, but the mind governed by the Spirit is life and peace. Rom 8:6

When God calls you from the back side of obscurity, to the forefront of the kingdom and you insert the key to your mind;

- ✓ There is no man on earth.
- ✓ No angel in heaven.
- ✓ No demon in hell can keep you from what God has called you to do.

LET'S BE REAL

Through a series of events I came to realize that available to me was an incredible power I knew nothing about. I was a bit disappointed with the leaders I grew up under because they compromised on teaching the deeper things of the kingdom.

My wife and I now engage kingdom work and worship wholeheartedly living in freedom by the leading of Gods Spirit. Some may consider that a bit strange, but we now realize it's normal. We are no longer concerned with what others think. We know our Father is pleased when we do so.

God is pleased when you give Him your all. He doesn't want you to wait until you get to heaven to pursue all He's created you to be.

Who do you seek your reward from, God or man? Eph 6:7-8

Let's Go Deeper: We are fighting satan and his dominions, and we have the weapons, the keys to divine power to get the job done. They are already in position awaiting activation through each one of us. This leads me to understand that satan's domain has doors. His citadel has doors that are barred and locked. And guess what, every locked door has a key!

But who has the key to that gate? Who is it that can unlock the gates of hell? Sorry, not you or I. We don't have the keys to the gates of hell. We have the keys to the *Kingdom of Heaven, which opens locks and unleashes* kingdom power to overcome anything brought against it, or us.

When you activate kingdom keys, you unlock the doorway to your mind. You unlock a realm of reality that does not reside in this earthly dominion.

In other words: To focus on kingdom provision, not worldly conditions.

Remember: Do not conform to the pattern of this world, but be transformed by the renewing of your mind… Rom 12:2

Our keys allow us to:

- ✓ Lock and unlock things through prayer and through the giftings the Spirit provides for the modern day church.

- ✓ We use those keys to lock satan out of lives and to break bondage in the name of Jesus by stepping into the authority (the access) He provides.

This brings me to the second set of keys: The keys to death and hell.

Revelation 1:18 Jesus declared: "I am the Living One; I was dead, and behold I am alive forever and ever! And I hold the keys of death and Hades."

Through His death the gates were opened. The gates of hell can't prevail against Him or the kingdom because He broke the power of sin and death. That's the set of keys you and I will never have. His keys provided for our redemption and eternal salvation.

- ✓ They were bought on the cross.
- ✓ They were used to conquer the grave.
- ✓ They broke down the door to death and hell.

Kingdom keys bring forth all that is:

- ✓ Appropriate.
- ✓ All that is lawful.
- ✓ And all that is wholesome and acceptable to God.

Additionally, we don't have to live with sickness or disease. Healing was paid for at the cross.

Surely he took up our pain and bore our suffering, yet we considered him punished by God, stricken by him, and afflicted. But he was pierced for our transgressions, he was crushed for our iniquities; the punishment that brought us peace was on him, and by his wounds we are healed.

We all, like sheep, have gone astray, each of us has turned to our own way; and the Lord has laid on him the iniquity of us all. Isaiah 53: 4-6

As empowered followers of Christ, we don't have to live with the deception of the enemy. Health can be restored, addictions can be broken, relationships and marriages can be repaired, the deaf can hear, the lame made to walk, and the blind see.

Heal the sick, raise the dead, cleanse those who have leprosy, drive out demons. Freely you have received; freely give. Matt 10:8

All things are possible through Christ, if we would only grasp hold of His untapped, unrealized power for the church in this present today.

Things To Think About

- ✓ Have you been using your keys in the moments of opportunity God gives?
- ✓ Are you ready to step into the empowerment Christ provided for you?
- ✓ Are you willing to release kingdom resources in yours and others lives?

Chapter 6

HE SAID GO

And to the centurion Jesus said, "Go; let it be done for you as you have believed." And the servant was healed at that very moment. Matt 8:13

As a young man of eighteen years, I joined the military in 1978 and spent twenty-five years traveling and raising a family. After all that time God planted us in Abilene, Texas. After many years and a series of encounters with God, I finally came to the realization that He prepared, and called me for a divine purpose. I served in many ministries primarily out of duty and without any real purpose.

For so many years my impression of what a Christian should be was what I was taught. I had no knowledge of the authority that was provided to me through Christ. I didn't understand that I had in my possession the "keys", the divine power to access the kingdom and its resources.

This realization came to light when my wife and I were invited to a healing service at New Hope church in our community.

Bill Johnson, a pastor from California was speaking that night. I never heard of this man prior to the conference. He started talking about the moving of the Spirit in healing and the many miracles his ministry was involved in. This really intrigued me.

I had never heard anyone speak of such things with the passion he showed. He made a statement that really struck my spirit. He said, *"Being a recipient of healing in most cases is a result of some simple act of faith."* This reminded me of Jesus in His hometown described in Mark 6, "A prophet without honor." *Jesus was amazed at their lack of faith and could do very little but heal a few of the sick.*

Healing Came

About thirty minutes into the service he stopped and said, "there is a man here that broke his right ankle and has been living with a deep aching pain for over twenty years." More than forty men stood. Immediately, my wife started giggling because she knew what was about to happen.

Few people knew that I broke my right ankle three times in the past twenty years. Once on the ice, then playing racquetball and the third time skiing. Looking straight at me he said; "there is one of you here that broke his right ankle not twice, but three times. If that's "not" you, sit down." I was the only one standing. Mark 6:5 ran through my head at this time.

At that point I placed my right foot into the isle and back in, "a simple act of faith." In my mind I didn't want to be counted with those who lacked faith. At that moment I felt a warm sensation in my ankle. The pain I experienced for so many years was gone! I had an "encounter" with God.

He called me forward and said, "you were healed weren't you." He told me to do something I couldn't do before. I squatted down and jumped up and down with my ankles. This is something I would never do before. Often my ankle would swell up and hurt for days. I wanted to test this out, so the next day I played tennis for six hours. To this day there is no pain and no swelling. This was a very humbling experience. I knew there were so many others with health problems much greater than mine, but God chose me.

He could not do any miracles there, except lay his hands on a few sick people and heal them. He was amazed at their lack of faith. Mark 6:5-6

The Healing Gift

Shortly after, in January of 2006 our church for the second time held a Word, Power, Spirit conference. The guest speakers were Pastors Jack Taylor, Dr. R.T Kendall, and Charles Carrin. At every conference, for some reason the Lord prompted me to follow Jack Taylor around as a prayer covering.

At the last conference we held, as I followed Jack he turned to me a said, "brother, you know you can do this." I suddenly realized he was right. I replied "yes" I can. I had a reality shift.

Now to each one the manifestation of the Spirit is given for the common good. 1 Cor 12:7

One Word

He then said only one word, "Go!" I knew in my spirit that I received this as permission to lay hands on people and pray for restoration. As I did there came a revelation of a new truth.

Each one of us has the authority to use our God given gifts to minister to others. I knew this, but the truth of it wasn't real to me.

In Luke 10, Jesus sent out the 72 under His authority and power. Jack's permission imparted a measure of his anointing under which I was to operate that night. God wanted me to test drive the keys, just as He did with the apostles and the 72.

At that moment, I looked up seeing the face of a young woman in the back by the flags worshiping. I just knew I had to pray for her. The music was playing, people were in the aisles dancing and some were on the ground resting in the Spirit. It looked like a battleground and it literally was because the Lord was restoring all the enemy had taken from many people that night.

Making my way through the crowd, I touched a young woman on the shoulder and she went down under the Spirit, as did a young man standing next to his chair. I found myself catching people while moving through the crowd.

This is something I had never experienced before!

It was another "encounter" with God! I knew I had to pray over this young woman for "rest." I eventually made my way to her and as I approached, our eyes locked. When I raised my hand she started going down under the power of the Spirit. I ran to catch her and did just in time.

I found out later from my wife that this young woman was struggling with the pressures of being a new pastor's wife and mother. She was literally exhausted emotionally, physically and spiritually.

> *What I try to convey to people is this. We as Christians have an incredible opportunity to minister to others through the power of the Holy Spirit. This is a power largely unrealized!*

The Lord gave her rest for more than two hours that evening. What is most incredible is that I finally realized God provides these wonderful spiritual gifts to His children to be used for the restoration of His people.

That's what normal Christian living should be like. Walking in your gift(s) will bring great blessing to others, as well as to you!

God uses ordinary people to progress His purpose and plan. That's what we were created for, this is our purpose. In everything we do, we must strive to bring glory to God.

It's when you have an "encounter" with God, when you see Him as He is, your mind progresses to the next *level of kingdom reality*, unlocking revelations of new "truth."

LET'S BE REAL

I like the story of the little boy who fell out of bed. When his mom asked him what happened, he answered, "I don't know. I guess I stayed too close to where I got in."

It's easy to do the same with our faith. It's tempting just to stay where we got in and never move.

Growth is the goal of the Christian. Maturity is mandatory. Just as with a child, if they cease to grow a parent is concerned. When we stop growing it might be wise to get a checkup. Not on our body, but on our heart. Not a physical, but a spiritual.

May I suggest one?

A check-up for your habit of prayer: Rom 12:12. Your habit of giving: 1 Cor 16:2. Your habit of fellowship: Heb 10:25.

Remember, don't stay too close to where you got in; it's risky resting on the edge.

Everything in between is a preparation for the next "kingdom on earth, as it is in heaven", encounter with our God. Are you ready for your encounter? Are you ready for the revealing of new kingdom truths?

I Understand Them

In our ministry each year we go out to the streets of our city for what we call "Christmas on The Street." During this event in December, hundreds of volunteers literally invade poor neighborhoods for three nights with thousands of presents, food boxes, bicycles, and clothing.

One year our target area was a small apartment complex where refugees lived. Many had two or three families living in these small apartments. As we pulled in, children started coming out from everywhere. As I got out of the truck I was immediately surrounded by a dozen kids. They were so excited because they had never seen anything like this before. As I started talking with them I realized they couldn't speak English. They were all jumping up and down with such excitement speaking in their native language from Mozambique.

All I knew to do was hand gesture them to follow me to the toy trailer. As we walked together, I suddenly realized this is what it must have been like for Jesus when the children all gathered around Him.

As we approached the toy trailer I turned to them again and asked their ages. All of a sudden to my amazement, I could understand what they were saying! They were all at once shouting out their ages and what they wanted. Wow, this has incredible. God gave me the ability in that moment to understand their language. I couldn't believe what was happening around me. I was utterly overwhelmed. With tears rolling down my cheeks I took them one-by-one and had our volunteers get them what they wanted for Christmas.

When each child was taken care of, I watched them gather together in the street excitedly opening their gifts. Suddenly as I was listening to them, I once again heard them all at the same time change from English to their native language.

When they heard this sound, a crowd came together in bewilderment, because each one heard their own language being spoken. Acts 2:6

For me the word bewildered was an understatement! God gave the understanding of different languages in both the Old and New Testaments. He is so amazing. It doesn't matter to Him what you may or may not know, or what you think you can or cannot do. He knows everything. God will provide a way to minister to others no matter what the obstacle might be.

The Holy Spirit searches the heart of every person and knows their motive (1 Corinthians 4:5). When He sees the motive of your heart as you engage those who have a need, He is a gracious Father who can and will make a way.

Once again, I had an "encounter" with God that I will never forget. In that moment I saw Him "as He really is" and it changed my life forever!

Things To Think About

- ✓ Have you been using your kingdom keys?
- ✓ Do you expect the kingdom to come in power?
- ✓ Are Spiritual gifts real to you today?
- ✓ Are you walking in kingdom authority?

See Him As He Is *Mick Brindle*

Chapter 7

The Stirring

Now, Lord, consider their threats and enable your servants to speak your word with great boldness. Stretch out your hand to heal and perform signs and wonders through the name of your holy servant Jesus."

After they prayed, the place where they were meeting was shaken. And they were all filled with the Holy Spirit and spoke the word of God boldly. Acts 4: 29-31

If you compare today to the early church, Christian living "is not normal." What is considered normal from a worldly perspective is in reality dysfunctional.

- ✓ Over time, dysfunction gradually becomes the functional norm.

What would happen if the Spirit moved freely in our lives without hindrance and this once again became normal every day Christian living?

It's when we live by, and walk in step with the Spirit, what was first established as normal comes more into perspective. As the Spirit moves in miracles signs, and wonders, as well directing your life path, that's when you start seeing Christ as He really is. Living and walking with the Spirit is simply this: "doing what's right according to God's Word glorifying Him." That's when we start to see the duplication of His ministry on this earth, just as it was during the early church.

When you see Him, when you "encounter" Him, you have become privileged. Seeing God at work is a glimpse of Him, as He really is. What God intended as normal was the kingdom coming in power; astonishing miracles, victory over the enemy, healing, deliverance, revelation; the kingdom in action.

Let' Go Deeper: You see, once you experience the ***"Realness"*** of God, you become responsible. Why? Because there is now an awakening in your spirit. You have tasted and have seen His glory, His goodness. When this happens there is a heightened awareness of the power and authority that He has provided. Your responsibility is to pursue more, to pursue Him.

What comes as well is a greater understanding of the kingdom resources available to you. The opposite is also true. He shows us how very little we have engaged in His desires and that's when the stirring begins.

It's in this awareness that a stirring takes place. This is an activation to become part of and engage His work! Many express this as a "calling."

Psalm 34:8 says: Taste and see that the Lord is good; blessed is the one who takes refuge in him.

> When we use kingdom keys, the kingdom comes more and more into perspective.

This simply means; when you experience (Gods glory), when you see Him as He is, you will crave and seek after the "greater measure" of His revealing. Your spirit will want more! Everything else becomes secondary. There is an increasing hunger for revealed truth.

This is why my life was so radically changed, because in my encounter I saw Him as He really is, when He healed me!

Now:
- ✓ When I touch someone they fall in the Spirit.
- ✓ When I pray, others are healed.
- ✓ When I have words of knowledge, they are revealed.
- ✓ When the Spirit speaks to me, events come about.

There is a progressive intensity for more of Him. We should be spiritually agitated by the lack of connection, the lack of awareness with the realm and resource of the kingdom.

Many have become spiritually discontent with what is considered normal Christian living. Nothing should satisfy the heart of a believer more than seeing the works of darkness brought into the light of truth and turned for good. Anything less should be abnormal and unfulfilling. Anything less is dysfunctional for a true follower of Christ.

Just as with the apostles and the 72, Jesus always empowers men and women for the work He sends them out to do. Why do you think they were so excited when they returned to Jesus?

It was because they experienced "the revealing of God"; they witnessed Him as He is, and as He worked through them! They were deeply stirred.

When you have an "encounter" with God, your spiritual awareness is raised to a heightened level. We need to catch hold of this. God reveals Himself to every believer "personally" and with a unique personal revelation of "Who He Is."

Provision Provided

Jesus made full provision for your forgiveness, healing in your body, and freedom from torment and affliction. Without minimizing physical healing, receiving Christ as Savior is the healing of the soul and most important because of the **eternal** result. This was the first awakening, or stirring of your spirit.

It doesn't matter if you are broken physically, emotionally, or spiritually, Jesus took care of it all. Physical healing is part of why Jesus went to the cross. We need to grasp hold of this, engage it, and by doing so, we can positively affect the spiritual position of the church in this day.

Church Perspectives

Today God is changing with greater momentum giving greater wisdom in the way we engage kingdom truth.

Let's Go Deeper: Beginning is a new shifting in what we accept as a *possibility*. The Holy Spirit is teaching his willing anointed to pursue life and ministry from a kingdom minded perspective resulting in a greater reality of heaven's power on earth.

A Deception

2 Cor 4, says the god of this world (the devil) has blinded the minds of unbelievers from the light (or truth) of the Gospel and the glory of Christ revealed in God.

And even if our gospel is veiled, it is veiled to those who are perishing. The god of this age has blinded the minds of unbelievers, so that they cannot see the light of the gospel that displays the glory of Christ, who is the image of God. 2 Cor 4:3-4

If you can hide or veil something, it means you can put it wherever you want. It's impossible to hide something that's everywhere all the time! The enemy can't stop God from being God. He can't hide God because he can't move Him. If you can move something, that means you have control. But the glory of God breaks through the veil of darkness. The light of truth pushes through the cracks of evil.

You see, the devil can't hide God, because God is Omnipresent. The only hope he has is to veil your eyes from the truth, or to deceive your mind.

His goal is to get our minds focused, distracted by the things of this earth, to keep us from seeing God's glory as He truly is.

✓ That's a form of Spiritual blindness!

In the church body today, there is a perspective on Spiritual gifts that many consider truth, but actually is a deception or veil put in place by the enemy. This deception is the belief that the gifts of the Spirit ended when the last apostle died in a time long ago and using these gifts were not for this modern day! I cannot express to you how much of a lie that truly is.

In 1 Corinthians 1:12, Paul writes that we should not be "uninformed" about the gifts of the Spirit. So, if we are to be informed, why would they not be for today?

I want to address this false perception or a spiritual blindness I call a "mindset" about the use of these gifts God provides. The Holy Spirit distributes spiritual gifts to each of us for the purpose of building one another up.

I believe God is reigniting the gifts for this reason. It's time to rebuild kingdom mindedness in the modern day church.

They are meant to bring about unity, healing, and a developed fullness in Christ. There is tremendous power in the use of these gifts provided, as you will see.

But to each one of us grace has been given as Christ apportioned it. This is why it says: "When he ascended on high, he led captives in his train and gave gifts to men." (What does "he ascended" mean except that he also descended to the lower, earthly regions? He who descended is the very one who ascended higher than all the heavens, in order to fill the whole universe.)

It was he who gave some to be apostles, some to be prophets, some to be evangelists, and some to be pastors and teachers, to prepare God's people for works of service, so that the body of Christ may be <u>built up</u> until we all reach unity in the faith and in the knowledge of the Son of God and become mature, attaining to **the whole measure of the fullness of Christ.** *Ephesians 4: 7-13*

A developing revelation
of who He is.

It's unavoidable that the Spirit will move more with increasing power as we approach the revealing of Christ. (His second coming) Acts 2:17 says, His Spirit will be poured out on all people as the end of time draws near. This is a prophetic fulfillment.

3-Different Mindsets of The Church

1. *Those who don't believe.*
2. *Those who believe it's possible.*
3. *Those who do believe.*

Those that believe miracles aren't for today are under a veil of deception. They have been blinded from truth!

Another group has a mindset of possibility and believes miracles are for today, but have a spirit of fearfulness when it comes to pursuing the unknown, the spiritual realm. This can be further expanded to include a fearfulness of what it might become! Most prevalently, leaders fear that emotions will take over and people will act out in the flesh, instead of trusting in the power and movement of the Holy Spirit.

It's been my experience that they're uncomfortable with a bunch of anointed people engaging the Spirit through the activation of their gifts. We must recognize that as the Spirit moves (a shift) occurs, making way for the unexpected under the power of His presence. This group is fearful when it comes to the power of God. Why, because they have no experience with it. It's when you experience a demonstration of power that the revelation of truth comes, and with it the stirring begins.

The final group is a minority (those flames of fire) in the church body that pursue the Spiritual gifts in this day. Their minds are set in belief because they know the truth. They are as Paul says; *"informed and engaged."* *(Emphasis added)*

It's in the pursuit that they experience the power of God with greater diversity in daily living and ministry. Their faith brings the hope of the kingdom (kingdom mindedness) into this present day. By faith they are confident in the provision of God and His kingdom.

Now faith is confidence in what we hope for and assurance about what we do not see. Heb 11:1

It's the middle group that believes in the gifts theologically, but become fearful in the pursuit. It's because of this fear that they don't experience the blessings that come from it. They present the greatest challenge of resistance when it comes to changing the mindset about the gifts of the Spirit in the church of today.

What I have discovered is that all three of these views exist in every congregation to some level! As I reflect back, in my travels I remember asking if I could pray for healing in a circumstance or illness. A common response was, they don't believe God works in such ways today and didn't want any of that power of the Spirit nonsense. Jesus always went about helping and doing good for people. He healed those who were oppressed and afflicted.

I have never read in Scripture about Jesus afflicting someone with sickness or disease! This goes against His very nature. Jesus came to restore and set captives free breaking the chains of spiritual and physical bondage!

LET'S BE REAL

Seriously, have you ever put God in a box? I know I have, mainly because that's what I was taught to do.

Unfortunately there are Spirit filled folks in every church that are kept in a box as well. It's been my experience that they are too intimidated by leadership to come out of the box and when they do they can expect a stern correction.

You know what that's called, squelching or hindering God's Spirit!

It's outright legalism and spiritual bullying. I've had my fill of it! Don't make the mistake of getting sucked into it. It's nothing but a black hole that leads to heartache and disappointment.

Where the Spirit of the Lord is there is freedom. 2 Cor 3:17

If you're not experiencing a loving, nurturing, freedom filled, grace giving place to grow, FIND one!

In the early church, Gods people knew this profound truth. Why, because they witnessed it in the ministry of Jesus, that of the apostles, and experienced it in their own Christian life. They walked with the Spirit. They did what Jesus did.

News about him spread all over Syria, and people brought to him all who were ill with various diseases, those suffering severe pain, the demon-possessed, those having seizures, and the paralyzed, and he healed them. Matt 4:24

Jesus knew what it meant to use kingdom keys unlocking kingdom provision.

Why? As I shared before, He saw His Father do the very same thing.

Jesus gave them this answer: "Very truly I tell you, the Son can do nothing by himself; he can do only what he sees his Father doing, because whatever the Father does the Son also does. For the Father loves the Son and shows him all he does. John 5: 19-20

For The One

In 1990 we lived in North Dakota and attended a rural church of about 300 members. One of our outreach ministries was to support four other churches without pastors in remote areas and preach each Sunday. I was asked to go to a little church on an Indian reservation at Devils Lake.

This was the first time I prepared and preached a message. Afterwards I thought I was ready for anything and started out on my forty-five minute drive to Devils Lake. The congregation was already gathered when I arrived. We sang a few songs and then I presented my message. At the end, I gave an invitation to receive Jesus. To my amazement half of those in attendance came forward.

But what I didn't mention was there were only two attending that morning. I wondered about this for some time. After asking God why there were so few who came that morning He told me this. I was sent for the one who would encounter Him that day and secure eternity. What a simply powerful answer. He also showed me that for the first time ever preaching I did very well. Half the church came for salvation. God has such a great sense of humor!

But what if I hadn't gone? What would have happened to that one man who received Jesus? I think we both had an encounter. We both saw Jesus as He really is, in that moment. The heart of the Father is to go after the one!

Things To Think About

- ✓ Is there a stirring within you for a deeper spiritual life?
- ✓ Is your mind focused on kingdom possibilities?
- ✓ Are you expecting God to present opportunities to minister to the one?

Chapter 8

ON THE ROAD

As he neared Damascus on his journey, suddenly a light from heaven flashed around him. He fell to the ground and heard a voice say to him, "Saul, Saul, why do you persecute me?" Acts 9: 3-4

In Acts 9 we see yet another powerful encounter with God. God reveals Himself to a man who has dedicated his life to imprisoning, punishing, and putting to death all those claiming to be followers of Christ. This was a man who spoke openly murderous threats against the Lord's disciples.

He was the one who stood by and guarded the clothes of those who stoned Stephen, a man full of God's grace and power, who performed great signs and wonders among the people.

This man Saul went to the high priest and asked for letters to the synagogues in Damascus. These letters gave him authority to imprison men and women who belonged to the "Way." (Christians)

However, God had other plans!

As Saul and his companions approached Damascus there was suddenly a blinding light that forced them all to the ground. He heard the Lord say to him, Saul, Saul, why do you persecute me?

> *Saul had an encounter with the Lord. He revealed Himself to Saul just as He did with Thomas as you will see.*

Jesus Appears to His Disciples

On the evening of that first day of the week, when the disciples were together, with the doors locked for fear of the Jewish leaders, Jesus came and stood among them and said, "Peace be with you!" After he said this, he showed them his hands and side. The disciples were overjoyed when they saw the Lord.

*Again Jesus said, "Peace be with you! As the Father has sent me, I am sending you." And with that he **breathed** on them and said, "Receive the Holy Spirit. If you forgive anyone's sins, their sins are forgiven; if you do not forgive them, they are not forgiven."*

Now Thomas, one of the Twelve, was not with the disciples when Jesus came. So the other disciples told him, "We have seen the Lord!"

But he said to them, "Unless I see the nail marks in his hands and put my finger where the nails were, and put my hand into his side, I will not believe." John 20: 19-25

What Thomas was saying is this; I don't believe it! In essence he was saying; don't you realize we are being hunted; people are looking to kill us. I'm living like an escaped prisoner on the run fearful for my life every moment of every day. I've had enough of this and now you are telling me Jesus is alive and you have seen Him! Basically he was saying, I'm out, I'm done with this. But what he didn't know was a week later he would have an encounter with Jesus and see Him as He really is!

Jesus Appears to Thomas

A week later his disciples were in the house again and Thomas was with them. Though the doors were locked, Jesus came and stood among them and said, "Peace be with you!" Then he said to Thomas, "Put your finger here; see my hands. Reach out your hand and put it into my side. Stop doubting and believe."

Thomas said to him, "My Lord and my God!"

Then Jesus told him, "Because you have seen me, you have believed; blessed are those who have not seen and yet have believed." John 20: 26-29

Do you know how important you are to God?

Jesus came back again just to reveal Himself to doubting Thomas. That's how important you are to God. He wants you to encounter Him personally. God wants to reveal Himself to you and when He does, it changes your life! Thomas experienced a reality shift. He had a one-on-one encounter just like Saul.

Back to Saul

Now when Saul got up, he quickly realized he was blind. His companions had to lead him by the hand into the city and for three days he remained there praying.

The Lord came to Ananias, a disciple in Damascus, and told him to go to the house of Judas on Straight Street and ask for this man from Tarsus.

Amazingly, Saul in a vision saw Ananias as well. He saw him place his hands on him and restore his sight. Ananias answered the Lord saying, "I have heard many reports about this man and his responsibility in persecuting and killing your people.

But the Lord said to Ananias, "Go! This man is my chosen instrument to proclaim my name to the Gentiles and their kings and to the people of Israel. Acts 9:15

Let's take a look at a few key points.

First, here's a man who was very well educated, had authority, and was a Pharisee. Saul enjoyed hunting down Christians and I'm sure took great pride in his abilities and favor with the high priest.

What's interesting is this. From heaven there was a flash of light. In a flash, the Lord takes him from powerful to powerless, to the lowest point in his life and strikes him blind.

He was utterly helpless and feared for his life. He had to completely rely on his companions.

A Lightening Strike

This reminded me of a personal experience as a teen. When I was in high school I worked at a fast food restaurant in the evenings. After school I would catch the city bus to work. One evening as I was standing there, the sky clouded up and it began to sprinkle.

I was leaning against a metal light post at the bus stop. I saw the bus turn the corner down the street, and as I did, I stepped away from the light post. At that very instant, lightening hit the pole.

The white light was so intense that it blinded me even with my eyes closed. It felt like I had a thousand needles piercing me all over my body. If I hadn't moved away from that light post at that very instant, I know I would have been killed. To this day, I think of that incident every time I go outside when it's thundering.

Now I can't imagine what all must have been going through his mind. However, I do know if I were him, I would be reflecting back on all of the horrible things I did to Gods people and the lives that were lost as a result of my actions and hatred.

I know Saul must have been utterly terrified of the situation he found himself in. But then he had a vision, a glimmer of hope!

Secondly, the Lord instructed Ananias to "Go" and pray for this man Saul. What Ananias didn't know, was how powerfully God would use Saul to impact the kingdom. Often we don't know how He will use us as His chosen instrument.

What intrigued me was this; the Lord revealed to him His purpose for Saul. Even though Saul was an enemy, Ananias went to this man. Ananias laid his hands on this killer of Christians and prayed for his healing. What an incredible act of humility and obedience.

> *God always gives us hope, especially in our time of desperation!*

Think about this. How hard is it to pray for someone you dislike or has done you wrong?

1 Peter 3:9 says; "Do not repay evil with evil or insult with insult. On the contrary, repay evil with blessing, because to this you were called (Like Ananias) so that you may inherit a blessing. 1 Pet 3:9

This made me ask myself; am I Christian enough to pray for someone who has caused me harm or even considered to be my enemy when (they) are in a desperate situation?

In other words; are you (Christ like) enough to truly love your enemy or those who mistreat you? To truly love your enemies places you in a position of complete humility and selflessness. But you know what, God loves that! Why, because Jesus did the same for us!

Jesus said, "I tell you, love your enemies and pray for those who persecute you," Matt 5:44

Saul, who we know as Paul, soon became an Apostle of Christ. He held a position of great power in the eyes of men. But God reduced him to helplessness and then brought him to the forefront using him powerfully to impact the kingdom for all eternity.

LET'S BE REAL

There was so much for Paul to consider. His past life, all the evil he had done, drawing pleasure from the way he destroyed lives.

His part in murder, torture, and searching cities for those claiming to be Christ followers.

I'm sure he sees the faces of women and children and all those he attacked without provocation.

In a moment, in a flash his life was changed. He believed in the way of the law pursuing it with all of his strength.

But then God! Paul hears a voice, he's asked the question, "Why are you persecuting Me"?

Think about this. How do we persecute Christ in our daily living?

Have we come to discover the realness of God? What about the faces you see daily?

It's amazing how God does these things. He often uses weakness to overcome those things that are strong. He brings us to a position of weakness to do mighty things in and through us. It's in weakness that God uses you in power to bring about tremendous results in the lives of others. But here's the key, we must be willing to do so without any regard for ourselves just as Ananias did.

We must be willing to step out of our areas of comfort (what we know) and step into the future, the (unknown) trusting God to do a mighty thing.

When discouragement or mistreatment comes your way, pray for another's encouragement and see what God will do, not only in their life, but yours too. Remember, always repay with a blessing, so you can be blessed as well.

Yes, Paul was a killer of Christians, but God made him one of the greatest preachers of all time. But here's the kicker. What if Ananias refused to pray for Saul's healing. What would have become of Saul?

Cancer healed

One Wednesday evening at church there was a small group of us that came for worship and prayer. Afterwards we were all milling about talking and just enjoying each other's company. As I was visiting with a group of friends, I happened to glance towards the back of the chapel.

Standing there was a woman I knew with some friends. As I continued to look at her she looked up and our eyes met. When they did, the Lord showed me that although everything seemed ok on the outside, inside she was struggling with something she wasn't willing to reveal.

It's hard to explain when this occurs, but I knew what she was struggling with wasn't a good thing. As I asked the Lord what it was, He revealed to me the word "cancer." At that moment I knew I had to go to her and pray for healing.

As I approached, she turned towards me and just broke down crying literally falling into my arms sobbing. As I held her, I spoke gentle words and reassured her it would be ok. She stated she found out today that she had breast cancer. I told her God revealed to me her newly discovered struggle.

She said, "I knew He would." She asked if I would pray for her and I told her the Lord sent me to do just that. I anointed her and her husband with oil and we prayed rebuking cancer in the name of Jesus.

The following week she went back for a follow up appointment to assess the type of chemotherapy they would start. After another complete examination, the doctor was dumbfounded. He told her she didn't have cancer anymore and that there was no trace of it. Praise the Lord!

I think many of us have encounters with the Lord or a prompting from the Holy Spirit. We at times may receive words of knowledge for others but don't always act on them. I can't help but know this happens more often than many of us are willing to admit. For most, the first reaction is to think that this can't be, and question whether or not it's really from the Lord. As a result we don't act on the prompting of the Holy Spirit. Those we were directed to will then miss the benefit of what God is willing to provide through us. God is always willing, many times we are not.

What would have been the result in this woman's life if I wasn't willing to move when God showed me her struggle? It really messes with your head when thinking about what I could have missed and the result of my unwillingness in her life.

It's very humbling when you actually follow through and then experience the result of what God just did. What a blessing it was to pray for her and then find out the next week that God completely healed her. This happened several years ago, but the experience is just a fresh today as it was then. A day doesn't go by without the Holy Spirit re-counting in my mind the many ways in which God chose to use me to bless so many, just because I was willing. I am so thankful I didn't "miss" it!

What if I would have said no? What would have happened to my friend? Remember God uses weakness to overcome the strong. Are you willing to help another even though it may be uncomfortable for you?

Are you willing to be used – To be blessed!

Things to Think About

- ✓ Are you like Thomas finding it difficult to believe the realness of God?
- ✓ Have you been presented with opportunities to serve another, but didn't?
- ✓ Does it take a lightning strike to help you realize God wants to use you?

Chapter 9

GENEROUS MERCY

A generous person will prosper; whoever refreshes others will be refreshed. Prov 11:25

This verse made me think about how often Jesus reveals Himself when it comes to His generosity and mercy? God also gives us opportunities every single day to do the same. After I read Proverbs 11:25, I really gave this serious thought. Could it be that we are as prosperous as we are generous? I believe our level of generosity to others directly determines our own prosperity, the (blessings) we receive, and the joy we have in our own lives.

Generosity is often described as how liberal we are in our giving and sharing what we have. In part this is true, but it's also related to how we share ourselves with others. It's the kindness and words of encouragement we share, not only with those we serve, but those we "serve with."

Being generous means being liberal in our giving or sharing. It's being unselfish in our actions towards others, free from meanness or smallness of mind or character.

Tears of Desperation

Recently I went to my bank to have a new debit card made because mine was cracked. As I walked in I noticed the lobby was full of customers waiting to see a member services representative. I didn't know if I should stay or come back another day. Then the Lord spoke to me and said, "Come back tomorrow." So I came back the next morning and discovered I was the only one in the lobby.

As I sat there waiting, I noticed there was one representative in her office with the light on. She came out and greeted me and we went to her office. I explained my reason for coming and she pulled up my account. As she was verifying my information, she noticed that my email said "Pastor Mick." She asked if I was a pastor and I said yes. She then said, "thank you God for sending me a pastor." Then I realized why God had me come back. I knew I was there for her.

All of a sudden she started telling me about everything going on in her life. She said her husband passed away several years ago, and that her teen daughter just had a baby. They were bringing the baby home the next day, but she was unprepared for the financial needs of helping to raise a grandchild. Throughout the conversation I was trying to bring encouragement the best I could and noticed that as she was telling me these things she was on the verge of tears.

As she finished helping me, I asked her if it would ok to pray for her and her daughter before leaving. And that's when it happened. She broke down weeping over her situation. Through her tears she said, "I've been asking God to send someone to pray for me."

Now I can't help but know that God orchestrated this whole encounter. I know that lobby was full the day before because the Lord wanted me to spend time ministering to this lady one-on-one the next morning. He wanted me to be generous with my mercy.

This is why it's so important to be in close relationship with the Lord. If I wasn't, I wouldn't have followed the Holy Spirit's direction to return the next day. I would have missed this incredible opportunity to be merciful to someone in a desperate situation. We were both tremendously blessed!

You see, that's what being generous with self is about. It's giving a part of yourself to another; it's bringing refreshment in the circumstance of someone's life without any regard for your own. I believe we saw Jesus "as He really is" in that moment.

Think about this. How often have we missed opportunities to show kindness to one another or have been the recipient of discouragement from those we serve, or maybe from someone we serve and work with?

Proverbs 15:4 says "Kind words heal and help; cutting words wound and maim. Another translation says a tongue that brings healing is like a tree of life. But a tongue that hurts produces a broken spirit.

This made me reflect on the times when I recognized the opportunity to build up someone's spirit, instead of breaking it down, just as in the case of this lady at the bank. It should be our hearts desire to show mercy as we serve and co-labor with one another, just as they did during the Lords ministry. Jesus showed humanity the ultimate act of mercy when all those in the city saw Him hanging on a cross. They saw Him as he really is. They saw Him as a lamb led to the slaughter, sacrificed for all mankind.

Most I'm sure as they looked upon Him hanging there, saw only a man. But those closest to Him saw the depth of God's love, so much so, that He sent His Son to die on a cross as a testimony to it.

Often I think we have become comfortable with the blessings of God in our lives and as a result, we forget to show mercy to those who have little, or are living in a desperate situation.

> *We don't know their story. Many times it's difficult to understand why, but that shouldn't keep us from showing mercy.*

It was the same for Peter on the boat. The boat was a place of safety and comfort. He knew what to expect on the boat because living and working on the water all of his life became normal.

Because we live in a blessed country, as inhabitants, we receive the benefit of God's blessing. Over time this becomes something we expect as normal and as a result we lose sight, we lose the understanding of so many that sacrificed for our benefit.

I know at times it's easy to forget about showing compassion, or to give understanding. I have to admit, I'm guilty of it. This reminds me of a story I once heard.

> **LET'S BE REAL**
>
> *How often have you not had time for someone and really just blew them off?*
>
> *Maybe you had a chance to speak words of encouragement to others, but were in too much of a rush to stop and share your mercy.*
>
> *I think we should be more like this little boy who understood the needs of this crippled dog. How about the farmer who took the time to listen and be blessed by the young boy's genuineness.*
>
> *Do others see your compassion and kindness or impatient tolerance? What does your family see?*
>
> *Showing mercy is love in action. What would life be like without mercy?*
>
> *Better yet, where would we spend eternity without Gods love and mercy?*

Puppy Love

A farmer's dog had an unexpected litter of puppies. He placed a sign on his fence that said, "Puppies for Sale." The little boy across the street saw the sign and emptied his piggy bank. He approached the farmer and said, "I would like to buy one of your puppies." He then poured his handful of change into the farmer's hand.

See Him As He Is Mick Brindle

The little boy asked, is this enough? The farmer said, "Let me see." So he counted it out and it came to thirty-nine cents. The farmer looked at him and said, "That's just right."

So he told his worker to let the puppies out of the barn. There were four puppies that ran out to the little boy. They were very playful. Then the little boy saw one puppy that sort of slid down the ramp. He noticed that the puppy had trouble with his back legs and couldn't walk very well. The little boy pointed and said, "I'll take that one!"

The farmer looked puzzled. He said, "You don't want that one son, he doesn't walk very well. He won't be able to run or play." Then the little boy reached down and raised his pant legs. He showed the farmer the metal braces on both of his legs. The little boy said, "I think that puppy is just right for me. You see, he's going to need someone who **"understands him."**

How often do we forget to show understanding, or lack mercy for another? What we really need to do is change our perspective. Sometimes I think we forget to place ourselves in others shoes. We see the same people day after day in the same situation and wonder how they can continually live the way they do.

What we don't always understand is why they don't change or how they got that way. That's when we need to be guarded about being judgmental.

Hebrews 4:16 says, Let us then approach God's throne of grace with confidence, so that we may receive mercy and find grace to help us in our time of need.

Let's Go Deeper: Mercy is showing compassion and kindness. It's not being judgmental of someone, no matter what the circumstance. It's showing others that they are "worthy" regardless of their past. It's showing divine favor and blessing. That's what God did when He sent Jesus as a replacement for our sinfulness. By doing so, God showed us His unmerited favor; He showed "mercy" and gave "grace." That's why we are now counted worthy.

Saved At 77

Frequently we take groups into poverty stricken areas for what we call a Street Feed. We hand out meals and drinks to anyone willing to receive them. Recently we took a group from Corpus Christi as an orientation to street ministry.

As they were going door to door, I simply walked down the street asking the Lord which houses needed prayer. He always says "Go." As He led me to the first house I knocked on the door and an elderly lady answered. I introduced myself and where I was from. I struck up a conversation about family and asked if she had relatives that lived in the city. She said she had two daughters and two grandsons. As she was speaking tears started welling up in her eyes. Obviously the Holy Spirit was starting to work on her.

With teary eyes she said, "My youngest grandson is a drug addict and I don't know what to do." She also shared that her husband passed away five years ago, and she was still grieving, and that she was also a cancer survivor of six years.

As we talked further I knew what I needed to do. I asked her if she knew Jesus and if He was a part of her life. She stated that she went to church whenever she could and read her bible on occasion. I said no, that's not what I'm asking. Do you know Jesus personally? Do you remember a time when you asked Him to be your Savior and Lord and to forgive you for all your past sins? Is He a personal part of your life?

She said, "No, I don't remember doing that!" That's when the tears started flowing. Before I left, we prayed for her family and she received Christ! She encountered God for real.

When God says "Go" He always has a pre-planned opportunity for you. It's His desire to use us to show His love and mercy to others.

Jesus was generous with His mercy. Why, because He takes the time to "understand" our circumstance.

How generous are you with your "mercy"? Do you just look at outside appearances or simply contemplate the situation others live in and not do anything about it?

Showing mercy is taking action, it's sharing the love of Christ with compassion towards others. I think we need more mercy, more action in the body of Christ in this day. After all, isn't that why we're here?

Things to Think About

- ✓ Do you speak words of life into others?
- ✓ Have there been times when others have treated or spoken harshly to you?
- ✓ Have you been a recipient of mercy, and if so, have you passed your blessing on to others?

Chapter 10

WOUNDED WARRIORS

"Come to me, all you who are weary and burdened, and I will give you rest. Take my yoke upon you and learn from me, for I am gentle and humble in heart, and you will find rest for your souls. For my yoke is easy and my burden is light." Matt 11: 28-30

What I see today are so many who are carrying wounds that debilitate their ability to even function in life. If they struggle to press through and live life, how can we expect them to engage kingdom work? There's such a great need for healing and hope in these days. Everywhere I go people are desperate for Gods touch and intervention in their lives.

Believe me, it's the Lord's desire that all be healed physically, spiritually and emotionally. His wisdom and love are far beyond our understanding. He knows what is best for us, but our eternal salvation is more important to Him than any temporary blessings.

The Spirit of the Lord is on me, because he has anointed me to preach good news to the poor. He has sent me to proclaim freedom for the prisoners and recovery of sight for the blind, to release the oppressed. Luke 4:18

Now the Lord is the Spirit, and where the Spirit of the Lord is, there is freedom. 2 Cor 3:17

There are times in His wisdom, that our healing or deliverance may be delayed. There will be times when our healing or deliverance may not come in a way that we expect. But in every instance of sickness, disease or affliction, our welfare and happiness are God's primary concern. He will never allow us to go through anything beyond what we are able to bear.

Divine healing is not just a speculative dream, it's a reality. The church is sick because we think, "well some are just supposed to be that way." Because we see so much sickness our perspective is, its "normal." Sickness is a curse from the enemy that comes against the church. Jesus came to break that curse and to set us free. Why do I tell you this?

- ✓ Because when we submit the things of God to the mind of man, unbelief and religion are the result.
- ✓ When we submit the mind of man to the things of God, freedom comes and a renewed perspective on the supernatural provision of the kingdom.

God's Glory

If God wants His people sick to bring Him glory, none us would be sick enough. That makes no sense at all. Why did Jesus come to destroy the works of the devil if sickness gives God glory? This would be dividing the house against itself. This perspective would be pitting the atoning works of the cross against God's will.

God is glorified when the works of the devil are destroyed. Jesus provided the power for each of us to destroy that work. Jesus came to destroy sickness providing for our wholeness and health.

And if God is glorified through and in Him, God will also glorify Him in Himself, and He will glorify Him at once and not delay. John 13:32

He who does what is sinful is of the devil, because the devil has been sinning from the beginning. The reason the Son of God appeared was to destroy the devil's work. 1 John 3:8

God Allowed

Some would argue that being sick increases our knowledge of God. This is the great deception. Sickness doesn't do a thing to increase our knowledge of God. Faith doesn't come from being sick. No measure of faith can be increased by sickness, because faith comes by hearing, and hearing by the Word. (Rom 10:17) Faith also comes by a demonstration of the Spirits power.

On the contrary, sickness prevents us from doing the will of the Father and that's what satan wants. How can you carry out His will when you're so sick you can't function? The only thing sickness teaches is that we don't want it.

I hear this often. My Uncle Bill was such a saint, but he got cancer and died. He read his Bible and prayed all the time. He did everything right in life, but was still struck down, I don't know about this healing stuff.

At times God miraculously heals, even the unbeliever! What we need to understand is that faith doesn't come by Uncle Bill.

> We can't use the circumstances of this world no matter what they look like to measure the will of the Father.

Let's Go Deeper: The will of God should measure the circumstances of life. You can't look at your circumstances and try to determine what His Word says. It's the Word of God that determines what the circumstances ought to be.

God's Will

Often I hear someone say they don't know what the will of the Father is. Well if confessing that you don't know what His will is, how can you know whether or not He wants to heal you? Faith for healing comes by His will and by His Word.

If you pray "If it's His will to be healed", this is actually a faith-destroying prayer, rather than a faith producing one. This is planting a seed of doubt. It's not "If" it's His will; the prayer should be, "I know it's His will" to heal.

"By His stripes we are healed." 1 Pet 2:24

This was to fulfill what was spoken through the prophet Isaiah: "He took up our infirmities and bore our diseases." Matt 8:17

God tells us what His will is. It's for salvation; "that none should perish" and that we be healed.

This is the will of the Father. Every provision for healing is already provided for. Every provision for salvation is already given.

A New Norm

Thankfully God is changing the way Christians think about the so-called impossible. He is teaching us to work hand-in-hand with the kingdom so the reality of heaven comes crashing into earthly problems overwhelming them. The results are astonishing miracles, great victories over the enemy, healing, deliverance, revelation, and more.

Many churches are starting to see the miraculous happen on a weekly, even a daily basis. Affliction and spiritual bondage are being vanquished by kingdom reality. God is showing us the "kingdom on earth as it is in heaven", as a new revolutionary approach to Christian living once again in this season. He's restoring!

God Realized

Normal Christian life should be miracles, spiritual intervention, and revelation. It brings peace, joy, love, a sense of well being and purpose. Written into the spiritual DNA of every believer is an appetite for the impossible that cannot be ignored or wished away.

The very Spirit that raised Jesus from the dead lives in us, making it possible for us to receive every provision of the kingdom.

We know in our hearts there is much more to life than what we perceive with our senses. Nothing satisfies the heart of a true believer more than seeing so-called impossibilities bow their knee to the name of Jesus.

The will of God is simply this: "On earth as it is in heaven." It's very basic and refreshing. This has been His plan from the beginning. When we pray this, we are praying for the kingdom dominion to be realized right here, right now.

This is a life-transforming way to "do" normal Christianity. What would happen if we all made this our mission?

Lives would be set free, bodies restored, the darkness lifted from people's minds, and the rule of the enemy would be pushed back in every way imaginable. Even beyond our imaginations.

Renewing the Mind

The only way to effectively "do" kingdom work is to engage the supernatural from God's perspective. The battle is in the mind. The mind is the essential tool in bringing kingdom reality too the problems and crisis people face day to day. God made our minds to be the gatekeeper of the supernatural.

On the mount of transfiguration, Jesus spoke with Moses and Elijah. The presence of heaven radiated through Jesus and He was brilliantly lit with the glory of God. His body revealed the reality of another realm.

After six days Jesus took Peter, James and John with him and led them up a high mountain, where they were all alone. There he was **transfigured** *before them. His clothes became dazzling white, whiter than anyone in the world could bleach them. And there appeared before them Elijah and Moses, who were talking with Jesus.*

Peter said to Jesus, "Rabbi, it is good for us to be here. Let us put up three shelters – one for you, one for Moses and one for Elijah." (He did not know what to say, they were so frightened.)

Then a cloud appeared and enveloped them, and a voice came from the cloud: "This is my Son, whom I love. Listen to him!" Mark 9: 2-7

Let's Go Deeper: The word "transfigured" in this event is the same word we find in Romans 12:2. The renewed mind "release's the reality," the presence, of another world in the same way Jesus shone with heaven's brilliance. It's not just that our thoughts are different, but that our way of thinking is transformed because of a renewed mentality.

A renewed mentality perceives (gives vision) from heaven to earth, not from the temporal (natural), to the eternal (supernatural).

Healing

This point I want to make very clear. Christians are absolutely responsible for bringing divine healing to people, ***"proving the will of God."*** This is bringing earthly reality into line with what's true in heaven. Remember the access we have to the "keys" of heaven. The miraculous is part of the normal Christian life.

Jesus, in His ministry emulated (displayed) the will of His Father. Jesus did what the Father did, and said what the Father said, just as we are to emulate what Jesus did. Why is it so easy for us to be fully convinced when we pray for someone's

---

LET'S BE REAL

Do you have a hole in your heart? Perhaps the wound is old... and you're angry. Or perhaps the wound is fresh... and you're hurt. Part of you may be broken and another part bitter.

Perhaps you've cried tears of anger that blaze in your heart like a consuming fire.

At some point you're left with a decision. Do I put the fire out or heat it up? Do I get over it or get even? Do I release it or resent it? Do I let my hurts heal or do I let hurt turn into hate?

Has holding on to hurts and hate done you any good? I think not.

Unfortunately, many hold on to hurts not willing to let them go.

Break the cycle, give it to the Lord and move on with your life!

He gave His life so you wouldn't have to!

salvation, that our prayer will be answered, and yet when we pray for restoration we find it difficult to believe they will be healed?

It's because salvation has been embraced and taught continuously by the Church for centuries, while the revelation of healing has not been widely received. For the most part it's been resisted.

Many believe that healing ended when the last apostle died and if you pray for the afflicted you are considered to be influenced by the devil.

Satan has done a great job of deceiving the church into thinking that sickness is from God to bring us closer to Him. Essentially, the devil and God have switched roles in the areas of sickness and health.

As you read and study the life of Christ, in His ministry, everywhere He went, He healed. It was always about restoration, joy, and freedom. Never once will you read that Jesus imparted affliction or sickness on anyone!

Conclusion

In Galatians 4, Paul addresses the believers there. What was happening is they were turning back to idol worship and legalism. *Paul said, I fear for you, that somehow I have wasted my efforts on you.* They were reverting back to a slave mentality. Paul asked; *have I now become your enemy by telling you the truth? (Gal 4:16)*

I think the obvious is right in front of our face. Most church leaders today rarely acknowledge that the church is wounded, that it's splintered in many ways. We are wounded in our thinking, our perspective, our direction, and in our obedience to following foundational principles established by God. He doesn't change. What was established from the beginning will stand throughout eternity.

There's a spirit of individualism and separatism when it comes to things of the kingdom. It's so obvious to me that when it comes to unity in the entire body, there's this shadow of spiritual blindness that rationalizes what many consider the direction of God.

In other words, "we are divided" because we do our own thing! I know these are bold statements and maybe a bit forthright, but it's the truth. As Paul said, "have I now become your enemy because I speak the truth?" I pray not. We have much to learn about this thing called "unity" as well as from one another.

It's only by the sovereignty and grace of God that He tolerates our self righteous individualism and self serving interpretation of His pre-ordained direction. The great thing is this; He is starting to dismantle the walls of division. As Christ's appearing approaches, this dismantling is an inevitable reality. It's a precursor to the eventual establishment of His physical kingdom on this earth. Praise the Lord!

I am so thankful He loves us with tolerance and allows us to come to ourselves, just as He did the prodigal son. He always gives us the opportunity to "see Him" even in the face of our own denial. When we "the church" are united in our pursuit with humility and expectant awe to seek His fullness and divinity; ***that's when we will see Him corporately, as He really is, and with power!***

This is when the whole measure of the fullness of Christ will be realized, when we the church body, once again, "Come To Our Senses.

Let us be a people who seek the face and favor of our loving Father. May we never cease to continually strive to "See the Glory of God."

Mick's Other Books

It's A God Thing
The Milk of Truth
The Kingdom Within
A Global Awakening
A Glow of Godliness
The Ministering Messiah
Releasing the Holy Spirit
Deception and the Destroyer
Healing Ministry Training Courses

Review At:
www.kingdomlinkministries.net

Made in the USA
Columbia, SC
23 December 2021